FAMILY 1739 IN ACTS

THE SOCIETY OF BIBLICAL LITERATURE
MONOGRAPH SERIES

Editors
Terence E. Fretheim
Carl R. Holladay

Number 48
FAMILY 1739 IN ACTS

by
Thomas C. Geer, Jr.

Thomas C. Geer, Jr.

FAMILY 1739 IN ACTS

Scholars Press
Atlanta, Georgia

FAMILY 1739 IN ACTS

by
Thomas C. Geer, Jr.

©1994
The Society of Biblical Literature

Library of Congress Cataloging in Publication Data

Geer, Thomas C.
    Family 1739 in Acts / Thomas C. Geer, Jr.
        p. cm. — (Monograph series ; no. 48)
    Includes bibliographical references.
    ISBN 0-7885-0036-8 (alk. paper). — ISBN 0-7885-0037-6 (pbk. :
alk. paper)
    1. Bible N.T. Acts—Criticism, Textual. 2. Bible. N.T. Acts.
Greek. Codex 1739—Criticism, Textual. 3. Manuscripts, Greek
(Medieval and modern) I. Title. II. Series: Monograph series
(Society of Biblical Literature) ; no. 48.
BS2625.2.G44   1994
226.6'048—dc20   94-34755
                                     CIP

Printed in the United States of America
on acid-free paper

I want to thank the staff of the Institute für neutestamentliche Wissenschaft in Münster, Germany for their gracious and kind assistance in the process of gathering data for this study. I also take this opportunity to express my appreciation to Dr. Carroll D. Osburn who introduced me to the discipline of New Testament textual criticism approximately twenty years ago. Because of their great patience, encouragement, and love through the years I dedicate this volume to Marcia, Sara, and Rachel.

TABLE OF CONTENTS

Family 1739 in Acts

Introduction

In the introduction to the the twenty-sixth edition of the Nestle-Aland text, Kurt and Barbara Aland summarized the current status of the discipline of New Testament textual criticism:

> The nineteenth century was the age of the uncials; the mid-twentieth century was the age of the papyri - this marked a striking advance over the nineteenth century. But now we are entering the age of the minuscules; their inclusion in textual studies contributes a new insight to the history of the New Testament text, and makes it possible to reach a sounder judgment of its original form.[1]

Since few minuscule manuscripts of the Greek New Testament are known with any sophisticated level of precision, whatever insights they may provide are still to be discovered, together with the assistance the minuscules might provide in determining the New Testament text's original form. Also, any attempt to chart the history of the New Testament text through the fifteenth century demands a far greater precision in our knowledge of most of the minuscule manuscripts than is now available. The material presented in the present study provides full information for twelve Greek minuscule manuscripts of the New Testament. This presentation hopefully will help clarify further the "age of the minuscules."

The several different levels on which manuscripts may be related to one another are the text-type (the largest identifiable grouping), then the textual group, and finally, the family.[2] Here, I am concerned with

---

[1]Kurt and Barbara Aland, *Novum Testamentum Graece*, 26th edition (Stuttgart: Deutsche Bibelgesellschaft, 1979), p. *47. Despite the recent suggestion that the Alands' claim was "a trifle premature," (See T. Ralston, "The 'Majority Text' and Byzantine Origins," *New Testament Studies* 38 (1992), 122-137) in general their point is correct.

[2]See E. C. Colwell, "The Significance of Grouping New Testament Manuscripts," *New Testament Studies* 4 (1958), 73-92.

the smallest identifiable grouping–the family. In my preliminary study of Family 1739,[3] I recognized that the family consisted of manuscripts 1739 945 and 1891. It was designated "Family 1739" because Codex 1739 is one of two of this group of minuscules (1891 is the other) dated in the tenth century and because Codex 1739 stands demonstrably closer to the Egyptian textual tradition in Acts than do the other members of the family. The material presented in this volume develops more precisely that familial relationship and introduces nine other manuscripts that are related to this family at varying levels. Information about these manuscripts has not been drawn from any previous listing; they have been identified as significantly related from fresh collations.[4]

The twelve manuscripts used for the present study are dated between the tenth and the sixteenth century; they are listed below by Gregory number and by date:

Mss. by Gregory Number		and by Date	
206	XIII	1739	X
322	XV	1891	X
323	XI	323	XI
429	XIV	945	XI
453	XIV	206	XIII
522	1515	429	XIV
630	XIV	453	XIV
945	XI	630	XIV
1704	1541	2200	XIV
1739	X	322	XV
1891	X	522	1515
2200	XIV	1704	1541

Ms. 1739 is a tenth century praxapostolos and is the best known of the twelve manuscripts. E. von der Goltz discovered this minuscule at Mount Athos in 1879, and though he made no definitive analytical statements about it, he concluded rather generally that it agrees with a

---

[3]Thomas C. Geer, Jr., "Codex 1739 in Acts and Its Relationship to Manuscripts 945 and 1891," *Bib* 69 (1988), 27-46.

[4]As the study progressed, however, I was able to compare the list with the information presented by Kurt Aland, *Text und Textwert der griechischen Handschriften des neuen Testaments III. Die Apostelgeschicthe. Band 1 und 2* (New York: Walter de Gruyter, 1993).

group of minuscules more than with major uncials, but that "agreements with the 'Western' text, such as D and E are not rare."[5] Von Soden considered Codex 1739 the leading representative of his I^{b2} group; thus among the general "Western" witnesses, but with more Byzantine influence than the members if his I^{a2} group.[6] Without specific analysis of evidence for Acts, Kirsopp Lake suggested that Codex 1739 may represent something of a Caesarean text in Acts since it "may well represent the Origenian–Caesaren text of the (Pauline) epistles more accurately than any manuscript in family Θ represents the corresponding text of the gospels."[7] More recently, Kurt and Barbara Aland have included this manuscript in their Category II in Acts, a category that includes "manuscripts of a special quality, but distinguished from manuscripts of category I by the presence of alien influences (particularly of the Byzantine text), and yet of importance for establishing the original text (e.g. the Egyptian text belongs here)."[8] Clearly, there has been a general lack of consensus about this manuscript. My earlier article demonstrated that this tenth–century minuscule is representative of the Egyptian textual tradition in Acts, influenced significantly by the Byzantine text and much less so by the "Western" textual tradition. More importantly, it is the leading member of Family 1739.[9]

Ms. 1891 is another tenth century praxapostolos and it is kept in Jerusalem at Saba. Most closely related to manuscripts 945 and 1739, it shares in common with Codex 1739 a basic affinity with the Egyptian tradition, although it is influenced in certain sections of Acts more

---

[5]E. F. von der Goltz, "Eine textkritische Arbeit des zehnten bezw. sechsten Jahrhunderts, herausgegeben nach einen Kodex des Athosklosters Lawra," *Texte und Untersuchungen* (Leipzig, 1899), 1-116.

[6]H. F. von Soden, *Die Schriften des Neuen Testaments*, Vol. I, Part III (Göttingen 1911), 1711-1714.

[7]K. Lake and S. New, *Six Collations of New Testament Manuscripts* (Cambridge: 1932), 141-217.

[8]Kurt and Barbara Aland, *The Text of the New Testament*, translated by Erroll F. Rhodes, second edition (Grand Rapids: William B. Eerdmans, 1989), 106. Kurt Aland, *Text und Textwert*, 545, indicates that 1739's highest level of agreement is with 1891 (89%) and 945 (81%).

[9]Again, that designation was chosen because 1739 is dated earlier than Codex 945 and as early as manuscript 1891, but not influenced as much as either by the Byzantine textual tradition of Acts. The original hand of Codex 1739 is not extant for 1:1-2:5 and thus that portion of the manuscript is omitted from this study.

significantly by the Byzantine tradition than is Codex 1739 (specifically, chapter 28; see below). Although von Soden placed Codex 1739 in his I^{a2} group, he placed Codex 1891 in his I^{b1} group. The Alands included it, as they did Codex 1739, in their category II for Acts.[10]

Ms. 945 is an eleventh–century minuscule containing the Gospels, Acts, and the Pauline letters and it is housed at Mt. Athos. Being most closely related to manuscripts 1739 and 1891 it is a leading member of Family 1739. It appears to have been intentionally altered to conform to the predominant text in the eleventh century; for the first seventeen chapters of Acts, it is statistically closer to the Byzantine tradition, while in chapters 18-28 it is more closely related to the Egyptian textual tradition in Acts. The Alands appear to be in some confusion about this manuscript; on p. 134 they placed it in their category III, while on p. 161 they put it in category II.[11]

Beyond the Alands' statistics, little is known about the other nine manuscripts included in this study. For that reason, in the following pages I present them in chronological order and provide only a few details about each manscript's date, contents, location, and any general comments made about it in earlier studies. In the latter part of the study, more specific conclusions will be provided for each of them. The Alands' categories from their handbook and Kurt Aland's figures in the Acts volume of *Text und Textwert* serve as a point of departure in the introduction. Chapters One and Two of this volume present the most complete information available about this group of manuscripts.

Ms. 323 is an eleventh–century praxapostolos that is held in Geneva at the Bibliothèque Publique et Universitaire. Von Soden put it in his I^{b2} group. The Alands have suggested that it may be a "sister manuscript" to Codex 322 and they place it in their category III.[12]

Ms. 206, in the British Library, is a thirteenth–century minuscule, containing Acts and the Pauline letters. Von Soden included

---

[10]Kurt and Barbara Aland, *The Text of the New Testament*, 136. Kurt Aland, *Text und Textwert*, 663, indicates that 1891's most significant level of agreement is with 1739 (94%), followed by 2200 (82%) and 945 (80%).

[11]Kurt and Barbara Aland, *The Text of the New Testament*. Kurt Aland, *Text und Textwert*, shows its highest level of agreement is with 1704 (87%) and 1739 (86%).

[12]Kurt and Barbara Aland, *The Text of the New Testament*, 132. Kurt Aland, *Text und Textwert*, 194, says that 323 has a 96% level of agreement with 322.

it in his I[b1] category, while the Alands put it in their category V for Acts.[13]

Ms. 429 is a fourteenth–century minuscule containing Acts, the Pauline letters, and Revelation. Is is in Wolfenbüttel at the Herzog August Bibliothek. The Alands placed it in their category III;[14] Von Soden included it in his I[b1] group.

Ms. 453 is a fourteenth–century minuscule containing only Acts and it is in Rome at the Vatican Library. Von Soden listed it among the manuscripts of his I[a1] group and the Alands put it in their category III.[15]

Ms. 630 is a fourteenth–century praxapostolos. It too is in the Vatican Library in Rome. The Alands categorized it as category III.[16]

Ms. 2200 is a fourteenth–century minuscule containing the entire New Testament. It is in Greece, at Elasson in Olympiotisses. The Alands placed it in their category III.[17]

Ms. 322 is a fifteenth–century praxapostolos, housed at the British Library in London. The Alands called it a "sister manuscript" to Codex 323 and they included it in their category III.[18]

Ms. 522, dated 1515, is in the Bodleian Library in Oxford and contains the whole New Testament. Along with 206 and 429, von

---

[13]Kurt and Barbara Aland, *The Text of the New Testament*, 132. Kurt Aland, *Text und Textwert*, 158, shows that its highest affinities are with 429 (94%) and 522 (90%).

[14]Kurt and Barbara Aland, *The Text of the New Testament*, 133. Kurt Aland, *Text und Textwert*, 214, indicates a 91% agreement with 206 and an 87% agreement with 522.

[15]Kurt and Barbara Aland, *The Text of the New Testament*, 133. Kurt Aland, *Text und Textwert*, 240, indicates a remarkable level of agreement with 307 (99%) and 2818 (96%).

[16]Kurt and Barbara Aland, *The Text of the New Testament*, 133. Kurt Aland, *Text und Textwert*, 310, says that 630 agrees with 2200 93% and with 1891 87%.

[17]Kurt and Barbara Aland, *The Text of the New Testament*, p. 137. Kurt Aland, *Text und Textwert*, 667, indicates a high level of agreement with 630 (93%), 1891 (93%), and 1739 (90%).

[18]Kurt and Barbara Aland, *The Text of the New Testament*, 132. Kurt Aland, *Text und Textwert*, 190, suggests a 98% agreement between 322 and 323, with its next highest level of agreement with 1739 (78%). In an earlier study, W. J. Elliott suggested that 322 was copied directly from 323. See W. J. Elliott, "The Relationship Between Mss. 322 and 323 of the Greek New Testament," *JTS* 18 (1967), 423-25.

Soden put 522 in his I^b1 group. The Alands put this manuscript in their category III in Acts.[19]

Ms. 1704 is from the sixteenth century (1541) and contains the entire New Testament. It is presently at Koutloumousiou at Mt. Athos. The Alands include it in their category III in Acts (V elsewhere).[20]

These last nine manuscripts are virtually unknown for Acts. The following pages indicate not only how they relate to the known textual traditions of Acts but also, more importantly, what is their relationship to each other in light of the already established Family 1739.

Methodology

By collating approximately one hundred manuscripts for the entire book of Acts, I have accumulated a total of 2838 places of variation.[21] This number excludes most spelling differences, itacisms, instances of moveable ν/σ, and singular readings. I compared the twelve manuscripts under investigation (along with several others) with each other at all those places of variation and then, for the sake of convenience, converted the figures into percentages. For instance, in chapters 1-28, Codices 1739 and 945 share the same reading 2561 times within a total of 2763 variations where these two are extant for Acts. That converts into a percentage of agreement of 92.7%.[22]

---

[19]Kurt and Barbara Aland, *The Text of the New Testament*, 133. Kurt Aland, *Text und Textwert*, 266, says that 522 agrees with 206 97% and with 429 94%.

[20]Kurt and Barbara Aland, *The Text of the New Testament*, 135. Kurt Aland, *Text und Textwert*, 519, indicates that 1704 has a high level of agreement with 945 (92%) and 1739 (83%).

[21]Obviously how one counts variation units will have an effect on final figures. An example of the principle at work in this volume is illustrated by a variation unit at Acts 26:1:

περὶ σεαυτοῦ λέγειν
p^74 ℵ C E 33 81 88 104
ὑπὲρ σεαυτοῦ λέγειν
B L P 049 69 105 181 325 MT
λέγειν περὶ σεαυτοῦ
H 945 1739 1891
λαλεῖν περὶ σεαυτοῦ
614 913 1518 1611

There are represented here two word substitutions (περί/ὑπέρ and λέγειν/λαλεῖν) and a change in word order. However, it is clearly one variation unit consisting of four readings and so is counted as only place of variation.

[22]There is no concern here to discuss levels of probability or significant levels of agreement as such, because the percentages reflect real numbers, not theoretical ones.

Particularly important at the first level of the investigation was the establishment of control groups with which the manuscripts of this study could be compared. While we are still awaiting full collations of all known manuscripts, the selection of control groups is a crucial aspect of ascertaining how newly studied manuscripts fit the known textual traditions of a New Testament document. The inclusion of inappropriate manuscripts within a control group can, of course, lead to great confusion and to incorrect conclusions.[23] I decided upon the control groups for the present study from fresh collations of manuscripts. Certainly I was aware of the generally recognized textual traditions in Acts, but the deciding factor was the level of agreement between certain groups of manuscripts that does not exist between others. Once the control groups were established, each of the twelve manuscripts was examined in relation to these. This quantitative analysis revealed some clear patterns among the manuscripts.

It has been recognized, however, that since the great mass of textual variation consists of minutiae, the manuscripts must be examined at places of *significant* variation to determine what types of agreements surface within these. The second half of chapter I, then, is a presentation of 147 "genetically significant" variations drawn from eight chapters of Acts. Within these variations there are readings that are characteristic of each of the textual traditions in Acts and these allow a more specific profile of each manuscript to emerge. When the twelve manuscripts were examined at those places, particularly taking notice of how they relate to the clear textual traditions, an even clearer profile of their affinities resulted.[24] I must stress that I attempted to

[23]This can be illustrated by the frequent use of Codex 33 as a member of a control group for the Alexandrian/Egyptian textual tradition in Acts. I have demonstrated in an earlier study that this manuscript is inappropriate in such contexts because its textual complexion changes toward the end of Acts 11. See Thomas C. Geer, Jr., "The Two Faces of Codex 33 in Acts," *NovT* 31 (1989), 39-47. The manuscripts used as members of a control group must demonstrate a consistent relationship in all sections of a document with certain other manuscripts.

[24]This methodology is basically that suggested by Colwell and Tune in E. C. Colwell and E. W. Tune, "The Quantitative Relationships Between MS Text-types," *Biblical and Patristic Studies in Memory of Robert Pierce Casey* , ed. J. N. Birdsall and R. W. Thompson (New York, 1963), 25-32. The important suggestion to "weigh" variants after counting them was an advance on their method made by Gordon Fee in G. D. Fee, "Codex Sinaiticus in the Gospel of John: A Contribution to Methodology in Establishing Textual Relationships," *NTS* 15 (October 1967/68), 23-44.

develop a sophisticated profile of these manuscripts only *after* the full quantitative analysis was made. A profile alone will never be able to generate the data necessary to classify a manuscript definitively. It can, however, further refine conclusions reached by the quantitative analysis.

Chapter II is a presentation and examination of the familial relationships that exist among the twelve manuscripts. The first level of this presentation is a set of charts showing the quantitative relationships among the members of the family for the whole of Acts, the two halves, and then various sections of the book. These charts are followed by others that show how those same percentages of agreement look when each manuscript is the basis for the comparison. Following these charts, I present two sets of readings characteristic of the manuscripts in the family. The first set consists of readings unique to these manuscripts; the second is a list of readings supported primarily by these manuscripts, but that also have some support from a few other witnesses.

The two appendices present data most of which is referred to but not presented in the study. Appendix I shows the number of times each of the manuscripts supports a particular type of reading (and also which actual readings) within the 147 "genetically significant" variations. Appendix II gives the percentages of agreement for each manuscript with the other eleven of the study (plus Codex Vaticanus and the Majority Text[25]) for each chapter of Acts. Since several of these manuscripts are cited regularly in NA[26] (323 453 945 1704 1739 and 1891), the information of the present investigation has an additional value in providing the basis for a more productive use of that apparatus.

---

[25]*The Greek New Testament According to the Majority Text*, ed. Zane C. Hodges and Arthur L. Farstad (New York: Thomas Nelson Publishers, 1982).

CHAPTER I

ANALYSIS OF THE TWELVE MANUSCRIPTS IN COMPARISON WITH THE KNOWN TEXTUAL TRADITIONS IN ACTS

Delineation of Control Groups

The first step in identifying the manuscripts' relationships to previously–known groupings in Acts is to determine sets of control groups for Acts for each of the textual traditions of that document. It matters little how one designates these groups;[1] the percentages of agreement make it very clear that some manuscripts agree with certain other ones significantly and with other ones less so. However these groups are entitled, the phenomenon is what is important.

Table 1 (reflecting the percentages of agreement among these manuscripts for all of Acts) shows that א A² B and 81 agree with each other in Acts significantly and do not share that same agreement with D

---

[1]Eldon Epp is the latest in a line of several who have attempted to modernize the designations used for textual clusters. See Eldon J. Epp, "The Significance of the Papyri for Determining the Nature of the New Testament Text in the Second Century: A Dynamic View of Textual Transmission," in *Gospel Traditions in the Second Century*, ed. William L. Petersen (Notre Dame: University of Notre Dame Press, 1989), 71-103.

[2]𝔓⁷⁴ is omitted from this select group for two reasons: 1) it is fragmentary and thus not a constant witness and 2) it agrees so closely with A (87.9%) that it adds nothing different to the picture. Its omission allows the use of a minuscule (81) from this same textual tradition.

Table 1
CONTROL GROUPS FOR ACTS

ℵ		A		B	
ℵ		ℵ	83.7	ℵ	85.5
A	83.7	A		A	82.6
B	85.5	B	82.6	B	
81	82.8	81	83.3	81	84.1
D	53.1	D	54.6	D	54.6
H	60.2	H	60.4	H	61.5
P	61.6	P	61.9	P	63.1
049	59.0	049	59.3	049	60.5
105	60.6	105	61.3	105	62.0

81		D		H	
ℵ	82.8	ℵ	53.1	ℵ	60.2
A	83.3	A	54.6	A	60.4
B	84.1	B	54.6	B	61.5
81		81	55.7	81	63.9
D	55.7	D		D	50.0
H	63.9	H	50.0	H	
P	65.4	P	50.5	P	93.3
049	63.4	049	48.8	049	92.9
105	65.2	105	50.4	105	92.1

P		049		105	
ℵ	61.6	ℵ	59.0	ℵ	60.6
A	61.9	A	59.3	A	61.3
B	63.1	B	60.5	B	62.0
81	65.4	81	63.4	81	65.2
D	50.5	D	48.8	D	50.4
H	93.3	H	92.9	H	92.1
P		P	91.8	P	93.9
049	91.8	049		049	92.8
105	93.9	105	92.8	105	

H[3] P 049 and 105. Here Colwell's well-known suggestion (that text-types are identifiable by manuscripts agreeing 70% with each other and separated by at least 10% from others[4]) is the easiest to attain. א A B and 81 agree with each other from 82.6% (A and B) to 85.5% (א and B), while their agreements with H P 049 and 105 range from 59.0% (א and 049) to 65.2% (81 and 105). On the other hand, H P 049 and 105 agree among themselves from 91.8% (P and 049) to 93.9% (P and 105) and with א A B and 81 from 59.0% (א and 049) to 65.2% (81 and 105). Because of the aberrant nature of the "Western" textual tradition in Acts, about all that is gained in the column under D is that Codex Bezae is actually slightly closer to the Egyptian textual tradition in Acts than it is to the Byzantine textual tradition. D is included in all these tables only for illustration purposes. Because of the unique nature of the "Western" textual tradition in Acts, it will be dealt with in a different manner.

These manuscripts (except D) represent the two most clearly defined groupings in Acts, which are designated as "Egyptian" and "Byzantine." The groups include early representatives of each type along with a minuscule representative of that same text-type from a significantly later period. There is little need to incorporate more manuscripts at this point, for the "lesser" Egyptians are simply Egyptian witnesses that have been influenced significantly by the Byzantine tradition and the "lesser" Byzantines are Byzantine witnesses that have been influenced significantly by either the Egyptian or "Western" textual tradition.

After examining these manuscripts in all known variations in Acts (Table 1), the next step confirmed the appropriateness of these manuscripts functioning as control groups in Acts. That second step is the examination of the agreements among these manuscripts in genetically significant varations in Acts. Over the past few years I have developed a tool that consists of 147 genetically significant variations taken from eight chapters of Acts (2, 8, 10, 14, 15, 18, 20, 24).[5] The

---

[3]Codex Angelicus (L) is not included in these tables, though it agrees significantly with H P 049 and 105. It was omitted because it lacks Acts 1:1-8:10, it adds little, if anything, to the picture given by H P 049 and 105, and its omission allows the inclusion of a Byzantine minuscule in the group.

[4]Colwell and Tune, 25-32.

[5]See pp. 29-63.

different readings in the 147 variations were designated either E[1], B[1], or W[1] (Primary Egyptian, Byzantine, or "Western", i.e., readings supported solely/primarily by witnesses for the one of the three textual traditions in Acts), or E[2], B[2],or W[2] (Secondary Egyptian, Byzantine, or "Western", i.e., readings supported by *any* significant witnesses for each textual tradition).   I then examined each manuscript under consideration at all of the 147 variations.   Table 2 shows the percentages of agreement of each manuscript with each type of reading. Within these 147 units of variation, when readings are supported primarily by witnesses of the Egyptian tradition, ℵ A B and 81 support those readings   from 87.5% (A) to 96.5% (ℵ) of the time. The Byzantine witnesses support those same readings from 0% (H 049 and 105) to 5.3% (P) of the time. When a reading is supported by at least some witnesses for the Egyptian textual tradition, the Egyptian control group members support those readings from 96.6% (A) to 100% (B), while the control group for the Byzantine tradition supports them from 59.1% (H) to 62.1% (P).   Clearly ℵ A B and 81 support one set of readings that are not supported by H P 049 and 105. In the readings supported primarily by Byzantine witnesses, we see, of course, just the opposite. Here, H P 049 and 105 support those readings from 82.7% (P) to 92.3% (049), while ℵ A B and 81 support those same readings only from 0% (ℵ B and 81) to 3.8% (A) of the time. The figures in relation to the "Western" textual tradition are very low among the members of these two groups, but Codex Bezae supports the primary "Western" readings 88.9%, the secondary "Western" readings 71.2%.

Table 2

	ℵ	A	B	81	D	H	P	049	105
E[1]%	96.5	87.5	93.0	88.2	42.9	0.0	5.3	0.0	0.0
E[2]%	99.3	96.6	100	97.9	39.0	59.1	62.1	58.6	61.0
B[1]%	0.0	3.8	0.0	0.0	8.0	85.7	82.7	92.3	88.9
B[2]%	56.5	61.6	58.2	67.7	30.5	99.1	97.9	100	100
W[1]%	1.4	1.4	0.0	4.0	88.9	0.0	0.0	0.0	0.0
W[2]%	10.2	13	9.6	10.4	71.2	13.6	13.6	13.1	14.0

The figures in Table 2 demonstrate clearly that ℵ A B and 81 represent one textual tradition in Acts, called here "Egyptian" and H P 049 and 105 represent another, named here "Byzantine."   Again, regardless of how one designates these traditions, they are clearly defined textual traditions in Acts. Codex Bezae is included as representative of the "Western" textual tradition, though it is certainly of a different nature than the other two.[6] Other manuscripts may later appear as good representatives of the text-types in question, but may be utilized as part of the control group only when they have shown the same level of agreement as the manuscripts within these groups have.

The Relationship of the Manuscripts to the Control Groups

To gain a sense of how each of the manuscripts of this study relates to the major textual traditions in Acts and to each other, the twelve manuscripts are now compared to the manuscripts of the control groups (Tables 3-5) and to each other (Tables 6-11). The following tables present the data for all of Acts, first giving the actual numbers of agreements at points of variation and then putting that number into percentages. How the specific manuscripts of this study relate to the control groups is of primary interest, but some of the better known manuscripts of Acts are included ($\mathfrak{P}^{45}$ $\mathfrak{P}^{74}$ E L 614 1175) to provide additional focus. Many more manuscripts have been collated and could be added to this list, but it would only introduce a great deal of later textual mixture into the picture. While that may be important to incorporate later, it is intrusive in the initial stages of the investigation.

The manuscripts most closely related to Codex Vaticanus in Table 3 are, as expected, א 81 $\mathfrak{P}^{74}$ and A. The most interesting aspect of this column is the relatively high level of agreement between B and 81, second only to א. The manuscripts under investigation (in bold type) fall between 72.7% (453) and 62.5% (322). The Byzantine witnesses fall between 63.1% (P) and 60.5% (049). D, as expected, is near the bottom at 54.6%.

Codex 81's column is very similar to that of B. One interesting difference is the position of $\mathfrak{P}^{45}$, which agrees with B 75.5% and with 81 only 68.7%. The manuscripts of the study fall between 75.8% (1739) and 65.5% (322). The numbers demonstrate that these manuscripts have a slightly higher level of agreement to 81, a later

---

[6]These groupings agree basically with the Alands' categorization of these manuscripts: They placed $\mathfrak{P}^{74}$ א A and B in category I; D in category IV; and H L P and 049 in category V. There is a certain circularity in the grouping process, but it is unavoidable. However these manuscripts may be designated as groupings, they certainly are related significantly to each other.

minuscule in the Egyptian tradition, than to B, an early uncial of that same textual tradition. That is to be expected, of course, since the manuscripts under investigation are themselves later minuscules. Again, as expected, Codex Bezae is at the bottom of the column.

Table 3

B			81		
ℵ	2418/2827	85.5%	B	1694/2015	84.1%
81	1694/2015	84.1%	A	1681/2017	83.3%
$\mathfrak{P}^{74}$	2042/2431	84.0%	$\mathfrak{P}^{74}$	1403/1687	83.2%
A	2340/2833	82.6%	ℵ	1663/2009	82.8%
C	1405/1791	78.4%	C	1149/1449	79.3%
1175	2217/2831	78.3%	1175	1582/2014	78.6%
$\mathfrak{P}^{45}$	262/347	75.5%			
			1739	1475/1947	75.8%
453	2049/2820	72.7%	453	1493/2007	74.4%
1739	2003/2763	72.5%	1891	1430/1923	74.4%
1891	1935/2739	70.6%	945	1461/2013	72.6%
945	1952/2829	69.0%			
2200	1782/2619	68.0%	630	1422/2005	70.9%
630	1873/2779	67.4%	2200	1362/1935	70.4%
E	1706/2618	65.2%	$\mathfrak{P}^{45}$	215/313	68.7%
429	1845/2834	65.1%	1704	1349/1974	68.3%
1704	1720/2660	64.7%	323	1358/2000	67.9%
323	1802/2817	64.0%	429	1369/2017	67.9%
522	1767/2783	63.5%	E	1214/1800	67.4%
P	1735/2748	63.1%	522	1332/2010	66.3%
206	1764/2822	62.5%	206	1317/2010	65.5%
322	1766/2825	62.5%	322	1317/2012	65.5%
105	1730/2791	62.0%	P	1263/1931	65.4%
H	1313/2136	61.5%	105	1313/2014	65.2%
L	1338/2204	60.7%	H	925/1448	63.9%
049	1708/2822	60.5%	L	1044/1643	63.5%
			049	1271/2006	63.4%
D	1056/1934	54.6%			
614	1518/2819	53.8%	614	1144/2002	57.1%
			D	679/1218	55.7%

Table 4 shows that codex 049 has a very high level of agreement with the other Byzantine manuscripts included here. The specific manuscripts being investigated here fall from 83.0% (322) to 65.1% (1739). Those are then followed by the witnesses for the Egyptian

Table 4

049			105		
H	1986/2137	92.9%	P	2543/2709	93.9%
105	2581/2782	92.8%	049	2581/2782	92.8%
P	2519/2744	91.8%	H	1933/2098	92.1%
L	1971/2206	89.3%	L	1984/2165	91.6%
322	2337/2816	83.0%	**322**	2406/2788	86.3%
323	2220/2808	79.1%	**323**	2285/2778	82.3%
206	2174/2813	77.3%	**206**	2242/2783	80.6%
429	2076/2825	73.5%	**429**	2122/2795	75.9%
522	1990/2774	71.7%	**522**	2033/2744	74.1%
2200	1858/2610	71.2%	**2200**	1924/2620	73.4%
1704	1877/2651	70.8%	**1704**	1917/2622	73.1%
630	1937/2770	69.9%	**630**	1978/2740	72.2%
453	1930/2811	68.7%	**453**	1958/2781	70.4%
1891	1839/2736	67.2%	**1891**	1864/2700	69.0%
E	1749/2608	67.1%	E	1765/2578	68.5%
614	1865/2810	66.4%	614	1899/2780	68.3%
945	1843/2821	65.3%	**945**	1885/2790	67.6%
1739	1798/2760	65.1%	**1739**	1837/2724	67.4%
81	1271/2006	63.4%	81	1313/2014	65.2%
C	1082/1779	60.8%	C	1094/1749	62.6%
1175	1709/2822	60.6%	B	1730/2791	62.0%
B	1708/2822	60.5%	1175	1732/2792	62.0%
$\mathfrak{P}^{74}$	1451/2421	59.8%	$\mathfrak{P}^{74}$	1471/2394	61.4%
A	1674/2824	59.3%	A	1712/2793	61.3%
ℵ	1663/2817	59.0%	$\mathfrak{P}^{45}$	212/347	61.1%
$\mathfrak{P}^{45}$	204/348	58.6%	ℵ	1688/2786	60.6%
D	939/1924	48.8%	D	954/1894	50.4%

tradition (from 63.4% [81] to 59.0% [ℵ]), and they are followed by D (48.8%). Codex 105, like 81, is included in the study as a representative of a later minuscule in its own textual tradition. Its level of agreement with the other Byzantine witnesses is high (93.9% [P] to 91.6% [L]). The manuscripts of the Egyptian tradition fall between 65.2% (81) and 60.6% (ℵ). Again, D is at the bottom of the column. The manuscripts under investigation fall between 86.3% (322) and

Table 5

D		
$\mathfrak{P}^{74}$	939/1680	55.7%
81	679/1218	55.7%
A	1056/1935	54.6%
B	1056/1934	54.6%
E	1035/1932	53.6%
C	645/1209	53.3%
$\mathfrak{P}^{45}$	156/293	53.2%
ℵ	1024/1930	53.1%
1175	1024/1934	52.9%
453	1010/1926	52.4%
1739	977/1867	52.3%
1891	950/1845	51.5%
P	935/1850	50.5%
105	954/1894	50.4%
323	970/1926	50.4%
945	971/1931	50.3%
2200	879/1748	50.3%
L	667/1328	50.2%
630	944/1884	50.1%
H	748/1495	50.0%
322	964/1927	50.0%
206	956/1924	49.7%
429	960/1936	49.6%
522	926/1885	49.1%
049	939/1924	48.8%
1704	874/1792	48.8%
614	932/1930	48.3%

67.4% (1739). While there is a great deal of similarity between the columns under 049 and 105 in general, the twelve manuscripts fall in exactly the same order under each, overall agreeing a little more closely with 105 than with 049. Again, this is expected since they, too, are later minuscules.

The striking thing about Table 5 is the limited amount of change from the top (55.7%) to the bottom (48.3%), a difference of only 7.4%. The unusual nature of this is evident when compared to the column under Codex Vaticanus where there is a difference of 31.7%, and the column under 105 where there is a spread of 43.5%. As was seen in Table 1, Codex Bezae has a closer relationship to the Egyptian text than to the Byzantine text in Acts. The manuscripts of this study fall between 52.4% (453) and 48.8% (1704), indicating an insignificant influence by the text of Codex Bezae upon these witnesses. A low level of agreement with Codex Bezae does not, of course, demonstrate all there is to say about that "Western" textual tradition, and this will be addressed in a more detailed examination later.

So far, nothing definitive can be concluded about the twelve manuscripts of the study. Some appear closer to B/81 (453 945 1739 and 1891), and others seem closer to 049/105 (206 322 323 429 522, 630 1704 and 2200). To clarify the relationships further, the next step is to see how these same manuscripts look as the point of comparison for the other manuscripts, particularly those in the control groups.

Relationship of the Control Groups to the Twelve Manuscripts

Table 6 demonstrates that 206 is more closely related to the later Byzantine text, agreeing with 105 80.6% and with the earlier Byzantine witnesses between 77.6% (P) and 74.4% (L). Its level of agreement with the Egyptian representatives extends from 65.5% (81) to 61.7% (‭א‬) and its relationship to Codex Bezae is very insignificant (49.7%). Its highest level of agreement is with other manuscripts of the study, particularly 429 and 522.

Table 6 also reveals a very high level of agreement between manuscripts 322 and 323, at 92.1%. Other than that high agreement with 323, 322's strongest affinity is with the Byzantine manuscripts, from 86.3% (105) to 82.2% (H). The Egyptian witnesses are toward the bottom of the column, extending from 65.5% (81) to 61.6% (‭א‬).

The manuscripts of the study, excluding 323, fall between 78.9% (206) and 71.8% (453).

Table 6

206			322		
429	2478/2826	87.7%	**323**	2593/2815	92.1%
522	2385/2779	85.8%			
			105	2406/2788	86.3%
2200	2112/2614	80.8%	P	2303/2745	83.9%
630	2242/2776	80.8%	L	1830/2201	83.1%
105	2242/2783	80.6%	049	2337/2816	83.0%
1704	2114/2652	79.7%	H	1755/2134	82.2%
1891	2167/2731	79.3%	**206**	2223/2817	78.9%
322	2223/2817	78.9%	**429**	2213/2829	78.2%
P	2127/2740	77.6%	**1704**	2075/2656	78.1%s
049	2174/2813	77.3%	**2200**	2002/2616	76.5%
945	2171/2821	77.0%	**522**	2116/2780	76.1%
323	2149/2809	76.5%	**630**	2101/2775	75.7%
1739	2098/2755	76.2%	**1891**	2035/2734	74.4%
H	1593/2132	74.7%	**1739**	2042/2760	74.0%
L	1637/2201	74.4%	**945**	2069/2824	73.3%
453	2007/2812	71.4%	**453**	2020/2815	71.8%
			E	1754/2612	67.2%
E	1731/2609	66.3%	614	1862/2814	66.2%
81	1317/2010	65.5%	81	1317/2012	65.5%
C	1148/1781	64.5%	C	1160/1784	65.0%
614	1809/2813	64.3%	1175	1811/2826	64.1%
1175	1808/2823	64.0%	$\mathfrak{P}^{74}$	1518/2427	62.5%
$\mathfrak{P}^{74}$	1539/2423	63.5%	B	1766/2825	62.5%
A	1786/2824	63.2%	A	1757/2827	62.2%
B	1764/2822	62.5%	$\aleph$	1737/2820	61.6%
$\aleph$	1738/2817	61.7%	$\mathfrak{P}^{45}$	211/348	60.6%
$\mathfrak{P}^{45}$	208/346	60.1%			
			D	964/1927	50.0%
D	956/1924	49.7%			

Similarly, 323 (Table 7) is closer to the later Byzantine textual tradition, agreeing 82.3% with 105. The earlier Byzantine witnesses extend from 79.6% (L) to 78.1% (H). The Egyptian witnesses are

Table 7

323			429		
322	2593/2815	92.1%	**522**	2538/2787	91.1%
105	2285/2778	82.3%	**206**	2478/2826	87.7%
L	1745/2193	79.6%	**630**	2367/2783	85.1%
P	2179/2737	79.6%	**2200**	2209/2623	84.2%
049	2220/2808	79.1%	**1891**	2295/2743	83.7%
1704	2063/2647	77.9%	**1704**	2198/2664	82.5%
429	2196/2821	77.8%	**945**	2301/2833	81.2%
H	1661/2127	78.1%	**1739**	2235/2767	80.8%
1739	2115/2752	76.9%	**322**	2213/2829	78.2%
1891	2097/2726	76.9%	**323**	2196/2821	77.8%
206	2149/2809	76.5%			
630	2109/2766	76.2%	105	2122/2795	75.9%
945	2141/2816	76.0%	**453**	2079/2824	73.6%
522	2100/2772	75.8%	P	2023/2752	73.5%
2200	1974/2606	75.7%	049	2076/2825	73.5%
453	2045/2807	72.9%	L	1603/2207	72.6%
			H	1536/2140	71.8%
81	1358/2000	67.9%			
E	1741/2606	66.8%	81	1369/2017	67.9%
C	1186/1777	66.7%	C	1198/1791	66.9%
1175	1853/2818	65.8%	$\mathfrak{P}^{74}$	1613/2434	66.3%
A	1820/2819	64.6%	1175	1881/2835	66.3%
614	1814/2806	64.6%	E	1735/2621	66.2%
$\mathfrak{P}^{74}$	1555/2420	64.3%	A	1858/2836	65.5%
B	1802/2817	64.0%	B	1845/2834	65.1%
ℵ	1786/2812	63.5%	ℵ	1824/2829	64.5%
$\mathfrak{P}^{45}$	215/346	62.1%	614	1788/2823	63.3%
			$\mathfrak{P}^{45}$	210/348	60.3%
D	970/1926	50.4%			
			D	960/1936	49.6%

clustered toward the bottom (from 67.9% [81] to 63.5% [‫א‬]) with Codex Bezae again at the very bottom. Its agreement with the other manuscripts under consideration falls immediately under the Byzantine

Table 8

453			522		
1891	2091/2730	76.6%	**429**	2538/2787	91.1%
C	1359/1782	76.3%			
1739	2083/2753	75.7%	**206**	2385/2779	85.8%
2200	1972/2609	75.6%	**630**	2287/2735	83.6%
630	2072/2769	74.8%	**2200**	2107/2573	81.9%
81	1493/2007	74.4%	**1891**	2197/2692	81.6%
1175	2086/2821	73.9%	**1704**	2110/2613	80.8%
945	2080/2819	73.8%	**945**	2211/2782	79.5%
429	2079/2824	73.6%	**1739**	2151/2718	79.1%
323	2045/2807	72.9%	**322**	2116/2780	76.1%
B	2049/2820	72.7%	**323**	2100/2772	75.8%
$\mathfrak{P}^{74}$	1760/2425	72.6%			
1704	1922/2650	72.5%	105	2033/2744	74.1%
522	1999/2773	72.1%	P	1948/2703	72.1%
322	2020/2815	71.8%	**453**	1999/2773	72.1%
			049	1990/2774	71.7%
206	2007/2812	71.4%	L	1542/2159	71.4%
A	2013/2822	71.3%	H	1473/2093	70.4%
‫א‬	2004/2815	71.2%			
105	1958/2781	70.4%	81	1332/2010	66.3%
P	1889/2738	69.0%	C	1160/1781	65.1%
L	1511/2196	68.8%	1175	1812/2784	65.1%
049	1930/2811	68.7%	E	1658/2570	64.5%
$\mathfrak{P}^{45}$	238/347	68.6%	$\mathfrak{P}^{74}$	1535/2386	64.3%
H	1445/2131	67.8%	A	1783/2785	64.0%
E	1754/2608	67.3%	B	1767/2783	63.5%
			‫א‬	1747/2778	62.9%
614	1713/2809	61.0%	614	1675/2774	60.4%
			$\mathfrak{P}^{45}$	205/347	59.1%
D	1010/1926	52.4%			
			D	926/1885	49.1%

witnesses. Like 206 and 322, manuscript 323 appears to be aligned more closely to the Byzantine textual tradition.

Manuscript 429 (Table 7) has a remarkable level of agreement with 522 (91.1%). The rest of the manuscripts of this study fall between 87.7% (206) and 73.6% (453). The Byzantine witnesses extend from 75.9% (105) to 71.8% (H), while the Egyptian manuscripts extend from 67.9% (81) to 64.5% (ℵ). D is again at the bottom of the column. This manuscript, too, seems to be statistically closer to the Byzantine textual tradition.

Manuscript 453 (Table 8) has no high level of agreement with any other manuscript included in this study. All that can be said at this point is that it is slightly closer to the Egyptian textual tradition than it is to the Byzantine tradition. It has all the appearances of being a very mixed text, but the degree of mixture can be ascertained only at a later point in the study.

Codex 522's high level of agreement with 429 (Table 8) has already been noticed (Table 7). The rest of the manuscripts of this investigation, with the exception of 453 (72.1%), agree with 522 from 85.8% (206) to 75.8% (323). The Byzantine witnesses are next, extending from 74.1% (105) to 70.4% (H). The Egyptian witnesses occupy the lower portion of the column from 66.3% (81) to 62.9% (ℵ). D is in its typical postion, at the bottom. Codex 522, like 206, 323, and 429, appears to be more closely related to the Byzantine tradition.

Manuscript 630 (Table 9) has a percentage of agreement exceeding 90% with two other manuscripts of this study: 2200 (91.7%) and 1891 (90.4%). Its agreements with the other manuscripts of this investigation extend from 87.0% (1739) to 74.8% (453). The Byzantine witness are next, from 72.2% (105) to 69.2% (L). The Egyptian witnesses occupy the lower half of the column, from 70.9% (81) to 66.8% (ℵ). Codex Bezae is, again, significantly lower than any others. In general, this manuscript appears to be more closely related to the Byzantine textual tradition.

945 (Table 9) has agreement surpassing 90% with three manuscripts, 1739 (92.7%), 1704 (91.0%), and 1891 (90.5%). Its level of agreement with the other manuscripts of this study fall into four distinct groups: (1) 630 (86.1%) and 2200 (84.6%); (2) 429 and 522 (81.2% and 79.5%); (3) 206 (77.0%) and 323 (76.0%); and (4) 453 (73.8%) and 322 (73.3%). After those, come the representatives

of the Egyptian textual tradition, from 72.6% (81) to 68.3% (א). The Byzantine witnesses are next, extending from 67.6% (105) to 64.5%

Table 9

630			945		
2200	2360/2573	91.7%	**1739**	2561/2763	92.7%
1891	2431/2688	90.4%	**1704**	2421/2660	91.0%
			1891	2479/2739	90.5%
1739	2360/2712	87.0%			
945	2393/2778	86.1%	**630**	2393/2778	86.1%
429	2367/2783	85.1%	**2200**	2216/2618	84.6%
1704	2206/2613	84.4%			
522	2287/2735	83.6%	**429**	2301/2833	81.2%
			522	2211/2782	79.5%
206	2242/2776	80.8%			
			206	2171/2821	77.0%
323	2109/2766	76.2%	**323**	2141/2816	76.0%
322	2101/2775	75.7%			
453	2072/2769	74.8%	**453**	2080/2819	73.8%
105	1978/2740	72.2%	**322**	2069/2824	73.3%
81	1422/2005	70.9%	81	1461/2013	72.6%
P	1889/2697	70.0%	$\mathfrak{P}^{74}$	1730/2429	71.2%
049	1937/2770	69.9%	1175	1985/2830	70.1%
$\mathfrak{P}^{74}$	1668/2401	69.5%	A	1971/2831	69.6%
L	1520/2198	69.2%	C	1241/1788	69.4%
C	1229/1782	69.0%	B	1952/2829	69.0%
1175	1916/2780	68.9%	א	1930/2824	68.3%
H	1461/2134	68.5%	105	1885/2790	67.6%
E	1757/2569	68.4%	E	1750/2616	66.9%
A	1877/2781	67.5%	P	1814/2747	66.0%
B	1873/2779	67.4%	049	1843/2821	65.3%
א	1853/2774	66.8%	L	1431/2203	65.0%
$\mathfrak{P}^{45}$	214/341	62.8%	H	1377/2203	64.5%
614	1711/2770	61.8%	$\mathfrak{P}^{45}$	217/346	62.7%
			614	1677/2818	59.5%
D	944/1884	50.1%			
			D	971/1931	50.3%

(H), and D is in its customary position. Thus Codex 945 appears to be more closely related to the Egyptian textual tradition in Acts.

Codex 1704 (Table 10) has a very significant level of agreement with 945 (91.0%), and agrees with both 1891 and 1739 more than 85.0%. Its highest level of agreement is with the other manuscripts of this study, from 91.0% (945) to 72.5% (453). The manuscripts of the Byzantine tradition are next, from 73.1% (105) to 68.6% (H), followed closely by the manuscripts of the Egyptian textual tradition, from 68.3% (81) to 64.1% (א). Codex Bezae is at the bottom, below 50.0%.

The column under 1739 (Table 10) is strikingly similar to the one under 945. 1739 has a level of agreement exceeding 92% with two manuscripts: 945 (93.0%) and 1891 (92.7%). Two distinct groupings appear at the top of the column: (945/1891 and 630/2200/1704). Then come the Egyptian witnesses just slightly higher than with 945, from 75.8% (81) to 71.6% (א). The Byzantine witnesses follow, agreeing from 67.4% (105) to 65.1% (049), and once again Codex Bezae is at the bottom of the column.

Codex 1891 (Table 11) has agreements exceeding 90% with three others: 1739 (93.0%), 945 (90.5%), and 630 (90.4%). Its percentages of agreement with the other manuscripts of this study fall into a pattern nearly identical to that under 945 and 1739. After those come the Egyptian witnesses, only very slightly lower than with 1739, from 74.4% (81) to 69.7% (א). These are followed by the Byzantine representatives extending from 69.0% (105) to 65.7% (H), just slightly higher than with 1739. Codex Bezae is again at the bottom at 51.5%. Like 945 and 1739, 1891 is more closely related to the Egyptian textual tradition in Acts.

Codex 2200's relationship to 630 (Table 11) has already been noted. Again, the manuscripts of this study have the highest level of agreeement with this manuscript, reaching from 91.7% (630) to 75.6% (453). There are three distinct groupings among the manuscripts at the top of the column. The Byzantine witnesses are next, from 73.4% (105) to 70.5% (H), and the bottom half of the column is dominated by the Egyptian representatives, extending from 70.4% (81) to 66.9% (א). As always, Codex Bezae is at the bottom, significantly separated from the others. Codex 2200 appears to have a slightly closer relationship with the Byzantine text in Acts than with the Egyptian.

Family 1739 in Acts

Table 10

1704			1739		
945	2421/2660	91.0%	1891	2535/2726	93.0%
			945	2561/2763	92.7%
1891	2234/2572	86.9%			
1739	2219/2593	85.6%	630	2360/2712	87.0%
630	2206/2613	84.4%	2200	2186/2552	85.7%
2200	2132/2527	84.4%	1704	2219/2593	85.6%
429	2198/2664	82.5%			
522	2110/2613	80.8%	429	2235/2767	80.8%
206	2114/2652	79.7%	522	2151/2718	79.1%
322	2075/2656	78.1%	323	2115/2752	76.9%
323	2063/2647	77.9%	206	2098/2755	76.2%
			81	1475/1947	75.8%
105	1917/2622	73.1%	453	2083/2753	75.7%
453	1922/2650	72.5%	𝔓⁷⁴	1792/2419	74.1%
P	1852/2578	71.8%	322	2042/2760	74.0%
049	1877/2651	70.8%	1175	2030/2764	73.4%
L	1494/2116	70.6%	A	2012/2765	72.8%
H	1375/2003	68.6%	C	1255/1723	72.8%
81	1349/1974	68.3%	B	2003/2763	72.5%
𝔓⁷⁴	1533/2276	67.4%	א	1974/2758	71.6%
1175	1773/2661	66.6%	E	1749/2551	68.6%
C	1114/1678	66.4%	105	1837/2724	67.4%
E	1612/2447	65.9%	P	1824/2748	66.4%
A	1744/2662	65.5%	𝔓⁴⁵	230/347	66.3%
B	1720/2660	64.7%	H	1403/2136	65.7%
א	1703/2655	64.1%	L	1442/2204	65.4%
614	1628/2649	61.5%	049	1798/2760	65.1%
𝔓⁴⁵	203/332	61.1%			
			614	1653/2752	60.1%
D	874/1792	48.8%			
			D	977/1867	52.3%

Table 11

1891			2200		
1739	2535/2726	93.0%	**630**	2360/2573	91.7%
945	2479/2739	90.5%	**1891**	2252/2533	88.9%
630	2431/2688	90.4%			
			1739	2186/2552	85.7%
2200	2252/2533	88.9%	**945**	2216/2618	84.6%
1704	2234/2572	86.9%	**1704**	2132/2527	84.4%
			429	2209/2623	84.2%
429	2295/2743	83.7%			
522	2197/2692	81.6%	**522**	2107/2573	81.9%
206	2167/2731	79.3%	**206**	2112/2614	80.8%
323	2097/2726	76.9%			
453	2091/2730	76.6%	**322**	2002/2616	76.5%
81	1430/1923	74.4%	**323**	1974/2606	75.7%
322	2035/2734	74.4%	**453**	1972/2609	75.6%
$\mathfrak{P}^{74}$	1738/2405	72.3%	105	1924/2620	73.4%
1175	1974/2740	72.0%	P	1813/2537	71.5%
C	1216/1696	71.7%	049	1858/2610	71.2%
A	1934/2741	70.6%	L	1479/2094	70.6%
B	1935/2739	70.6%	H	1358/1927	70.5%
א	1905/2734	69.7%	81	1362/1935	70.4%
105	1864/2700	69.0%	C	1101/1578	69.8%
P	1851/2724	68.0%	1175	1811/2620	69.1%
E	1710/2527	67.7%	$\mathfrak{P}^{74}$	1540/2234	68.9%
049	1839/2736	67.2%	B	1782/2619	68.0%
L	1471/2202	66.8%	A	1777/2621	67.8%
$\mathfrak{P}^{45}$	227/345	65.8%	E	1626/2408	67.5%
H	1396/2124	65.7%	א	1748/2614	66.9%
			$\mathfrak{P}^{45}$	208/330	63.0%
614	1644/2728	60.3%	614	1619/2609	62.1%
D	950/1845	51.5%	D	879/1748	50.3%

This initial quantitative analysis reveals that eight of the twelve manuscripts of this study fall generally into the Byzantine textual tradition (206 322 323 429 522 630 1704 2200) and the other four are slightly closer to the Egyptian textual tradition (453 945 1739 1891). This is, of course, only a preliminary conclusion. The next step is to refine these preliminary conclusions by looking more closely at a specific group and type of variant readings.

Genetically Significant Variations

In this section, I examine each of the manuscripts in light of 147 "genetically significant variations" in Acts. "Genetically significant variations" is a phrase borrowed from Gordon Fee, who described the phrase:

> Genetic relationship must ultimately be built on firmer ground than on agreements, for example, in the addition/omission of articles, possessives, conjunctions, or the tense change of verbs, or certain kinds of changes of word order, or, in many instances, of harmonization. On the other hand, major rewritings, some large addition/omission variants, certain kinds of substitutions, as well as several kinds of word order variants, must certainly be recognized as the basic data from which to construct stemmata of textual relationships.[7]

Obviously, there will always be a subjective element in determining which variant readings are genetically significant and which are not, but hopefully with the substantial number included here, disagreements over the importance of a reading or two will not affect the overall results. The readings have been drawn from a large cross-section of Acts–chapters 2 8 10 14 15 18 20 and 24. Each reading within the variations is considered "E" (Egyptian), "B" (Byzantine), "W" ("Western"), a combination of two or three of these, or a singular reading. The charts in Appendix I show how many and which of each kind of reading the manuscripts contain. There was no attempt to locate variation units where manuscripts align in certain ways; the emphasis is only on locating significant variation units. By seeing how

---

[7]Cited from Gordon D. Fee, "Toward the Classification of the Term 'Textual Variant," in *Studies in the Theory and Method of New Testament Textual Criticism, Studies and Documents* Vol. 45, ed. Eldon Jay Epp and Gordon D. Fee (Grand Rapids: William B. Eerdmans Publishing Co., 1993), 67-68.

many of each kind of reading each manuscript contains within those, it will be possible to obtain a clearer picture of its textual affinities.

It was extremely difficult at times to determine whether a reading was a "Western" reading or not. For instance, see variation number 61 (on page 41).

14:19b καὶ πείσαντες τοὺς ὄχλους–$\mathfrak{P}^{74}$ ℵ A B D E H L P 049 105 614   MT sa bo

διὰ διαλεγομένων αὐτῶν παρρησίᾳ ἔπεισαν τοὺς ὄχλους ἀποστῆναι ἀπ᾽ αὐτῶν λέγοντες ὅτι ἀληθὲς λέγουσιν ἀλλὰ πάντα ψεύδονται καὶ πείσαντες τοὺς ὄχλους καί–C 81 206 322 323 (429) 453 522 630 945 1175 1704 1739 1891 2200   (h) sy^{hmg} mae

Here D and E, two important witnesses to "Western" readings, both support the Egyptian/Byzantine reading. But does the support of the Syriac Harclean margin and the middle Egyptian qualify the second reading to be considered "Western"? Obviously, the reading has the "flavor" of "Western" readings, though its main support comes from the manuscripts of this study. To consider it "Western" involves circularity, for it demonstrates that these manuscripts are "Western" because they support this reading, which is, in fact, their reading. However, despite this obvious problem, such readings are considered "Western" in the following analysis in an attempt to allow that textual tradition as much influence as possible on these manuscripts, since some have been classified in the "Western" textual tradition. Generally, in the following textual variations, a combination of any of the following that seemed signficant was enough to warrant the designation "Western" for a reading: D E 614 it lat sy^h sy^{hmg} mae.

The following witnesses are presented consistently in the variations that follow; if one of them does not appear for a particular variant it is because it lacks that variation unit: $\mathfrak{P}^{45}$ $\mathfrak{P}^{74}$ ℵ A B C D E H L P 049 81 105 206 322 323 429 453 522 614 630 945 1175 1704 1739 1891 2200 and MT (the reading of the published *The Majority Text*, included to represent the broad Byzantine tradition). Where the MT and the *Textus Receptus* differ, TR is included. The fragmentary papyri are included whenever present. I have made no attempt to represent the versional evidence completely; the evidence presented here is that given in the NA²⁶ critical apparatus.

"Genetically Significant" Variations in Acts
  (in chapters 2, 8, 10, 14, 15, 18, 20, and 24)

1. 2:1 omit–א A B C D E 049 81 105 206 322 323 429 522 630
                945 1175 1704 2200 MT sa bo

       οἱ ἀπόστολοι–453 614 p* t

2. 2:6 τῇ ἰδίᾳ διαλέκτῳ λαλούντων–א A B C E 049 81 105 206
                322 323 429 522 614 630 945 1175 1704 1739
                2200 MT sa bo

       λαλοῦντας ταῖς γλώσσαις–D syᵖ· ʰᵐᵍ Augᵖᵗ

3. 2:7 λέγοντες–𝔓⁷⁴ א A B C* 81 1175   r vg sa bo

       λέγοντες πρὸς ἀλλήλους–C³ D E 049 096 105 206 322
                323 453 (522) 614 630 945 1704 1739 2200
                MT sa bo

4. 2:12 ἄλλος πρὸς ἄλλον λέγοντες–א A B C E 049 (076) 81 105
                206 322 323 453 (522) 614 630 945 1175
                1704 1739 2200   MT sa bo

       ἄλλος πρὸς ἄλλον ἐπὶ τῷ γεγονότι καὶ λέγοντες–D
       (syʰ ᵐᵍ)

5. 2:17 ἐν ταῖς ἐσχάταις ἡμέραις–ℵ A D E P 049 096 81 105
    206 322 323 429 453 522 614 630 945 1704
    1739 2200 MT it bo

    μετὰ ταῦτα–B 076 sa^mss

    ἐν ταῖς ἡμέραις ἐκείναις–1175

    μετὰ ταῦτα ἐν ταῖς ἐσχάταις ἡμέραις–C

6. 2:18 ἐν ταῖς ἡμέραις ἐκείναις–ℵ A B C E P 049 076 81 105
    206 322 323 429 453 522 614 630 945 1175
    1704 1739 MT sa bo

    omit–D   gig r

7. 2:19 αἷμα καὶ πῦρ καὶ ἀτμίδα καπνοῦ–𝔓^74 ℵ A B C E 049
    076 81 105 206 322 323 429 453 522 614 630
    945 1175 1704 1739 2200 MT sa bo

    omit–D   it

8. 2:20 καὶ ἐπιφανῆ - 𝔓^74 A B C E P 049 076 81 105 206 322 323
    429 453 522 614 630 945 1175 1704 1739
    1891 2200 MT sa bo

    omit–ℵ D   gig r

9. 2:23 omit–𝔓^74 ℵ A B C 81 322 323 1739 1891 lat sa bo   Ir^lat
    Ath

    λαβόντες–ℵ² D E P 049 105 206 429 453 522 614 630 945
    1175 1704 2200 MT sy^h Eus

10.   2:30 καθίσαι–ℵ A B C D^c 81 1175   lat sy^p sa bo   Ir^{lat}

       τὸ κατὰ σάρκα ἀναστήσειν τὸν χριστὸν καθίσαι–(D)
       105 206 322 (453) 614 630 945 1704   MT
       sy^h mae   Or

       τὸ κατὰ σάρκα ἀναστήσειν τὸν χριστὸν καὶ κάθισαι–
       429 522 1611

       ἀναστῆσαι τὸν χριστὸν καὶ καθίσαι–E

       ἀναστήσεν τὸν χριστὸν καθίσαι–323 1739 1891

11.   2:31 omit–𝔓⁷⁴ ℵ A B C* D 81 1175   lat sy^p sa bo   Ir^{lat} Or

       ἡ ψυχὴ αὐτοῦ–C³ E P 049 105 206 322 323 429 453 522
       614 630 945 1518 1611 1704 1739 1891 2200
       MT   sy^h

12.   2:37a   omit–𝔓⁷⁴ ℵ A B C P 049 81 105 206 322 323 429 453
       522 614   630 945 1175 1704 1739 1891 2200
       MT   it sa bo

       τότε πάντες οἱ συνελθόντες καί–D   sy^{hmg}

13.   2:37b   omit–𝔓⁷⁴ ℵ A B C 049 81 206 322 323 429 453 522 614
       630 945 1175 1704 1739 1891 2200 MT   sa
       bo

       ὑποδείξατε ἡμῖν–D E   it sy^{h mg}

14. 2:38 Πέτρος δὲ πρὸς αὐτοὺς μετανοήσατε φησίν–ℵ A (B) C
     (D) 81 522 630 945 1704 1739 1891 2200 vg

   Πέτρος δὲ ἔφη πρὸς αὐτοὺς μετανοήσατε–E P 049 105
   322 323 429 453 614 MT gig Ir^lat

   εἶπε δὲ Πέτρος πρὸς αὐτοὺς μετανοήσατε– 206

15. 2:41 omit–𝔓⁷⁴ ℵ A B C D 81 1175 it sa bo

   ἀσμένως–E P 049 105 206 322 323 429 453 522 614 630
   945 1704 1739 1891 2200 MT sy^{p,h}

16. 2:43 διὰ τῶν ἀποστόλων ἐγίνετο–B D P 049 81 105 206 322
     323 429 522 1704 1739 1891 2200 MT it sa
     bo

   διὰ τῶν χείρων τῶν ἀποστόλων ἐγίνετο–(E) 614

   ἐγίνετο διὰ τῶν ἀποστόλων ἐν ᾽Ιερουσαλὴμ φόβος τε ἦν
   μέγας ἐπὶ πάντας καί–(𝔓⁷⁴) ℵ A 453 1175

17. 2:47 ἐπὶ τὸ αὐτὸ Πέτρος δέ–𝔓⁷⁴ℵ A B C 81 1175 1704

   τῇ ἐκκλησίᾳ ἐπὶ τὸ αὐτὸ δὲ Πέτρος–E P 049 105 206 322
   323 (429) 453 (522) 614 (630) (945) (1739)
   (1891) 2200 MT sy

   ἐπὶ τὸ αὐτὸ ἐν τῇ ἐκκλησίᾳ ἐν δὲ ταῖς ἡμέραις ταύταις–
   D (p) mae

18.   8:1a omit–𝔭⁷⁴ ℵ A B C E H P 049 81 105 206 322 323 429 453
                    522 614 630 945 1175 1704 1739 1891 2200

       καὶ θλῖψις–D (h saᵐˢˢ mae)

19.   8:1b omit–𝔭⁷⁴ ℵ A B C E H P 049 81 105 206 322 323 429 453
                    522 614 630 945 1704 1739 1891 2200 MT
                    bo

       οἳ ἔμειναν ἐν ᾽Ιερουσαλήμ–D* 1175   it saᵐˢˢ mae

20.   8:10 καλουμένη–𝔭⁷⁴ ℵ A B C D E 81 323 945 1175 1704 1739
                    1891   it bo

       λεγομένη–614

       omit–H L P 049 105 206 322 429 453 522 630 MT   syᵖ
            sa mae

21.   8:13 σημεῖα καὶ δυνάμεις μεγάλας γινομένας–𝔭⁷⁴ ℵ A B D
                    81 429 453 522 (630) 945 1175 1704 1739
                    1891   gig p sa bo

       δυνάμεις καὶ σημεῖα γινόμενα–(E) H L P 049 105 206
            (322) 614 2200 MT

       μεγάλα γινόμενα–323

22.   8:18 ἰδών–𝔭⁷⁴ ℵ A B C D E 81 322 323 429 453 522 614 630
                    945 1175 1704 1739 1891 2200

       θεασάμενος–H L P 049 105 206 MT

23. 8:24 omit–𝔓⁷⁴ ℵ A B C E H L P 049 81 105 322 323 429 453
522 630 945 1175 1704 1739 1891 2200 MT
sa bo

παρακαλῶ–D 614   gig r syʰ** mae

24. 8:37 omit–𝔓⁷⁴ ℵ A B C H L P 049 81 105 206 614 1175   MT
sa bo

εἶπε δὲ ὁ Φίλιππος, Εἰ πιστεύεις ἐξ ὅλης τῆς καρδίας,
ἔξεστιν· ἀποκριθεὶς δὲ εἶπε, Πιστεύω τὸν υἱὸν τοῦ θεοῦ
εἶναι τὸν Ἰησοῦν Χριστόν–
(E) 322 323 429 453 (522) 630 945 1704
1739 1891 2200 TR   (it vgᶜˡ syʰ** mae   Ir
Cyp

25. 8:38 ἀμφότεροι εἰς τὸ ὕδωρ–𝔓⁷⁴ ℵ A B C H L P 049 81 105
206 322 323 429 453 522 630 945 1175 1704
1739 1891 2200   MT

εἰς τὸ ὕδωρ ἀμφότεροι–E 614

26. 8:39 omit–𝔓⁴⁵ 𝔓⁷⁴ ℵ B C E H L P 049 105 206 429 522 614
630 1175 2200 MT sa bo

ἅγιον ἐπέπεσεν ἐπὶ τὸν εὐνοῦχον ἄγγελος δέ–A 88ᵐᵍ
322 323 453 945 1704 1739 1891   l p (w)
(syʰ**) mae

27. 10:3 περί–𝔓⁷⁴ ℵ A B C E 81 322 323 429 453 522 614 630 945
1175 1704 1739 1891 2200 sy sa

omit–L P 049 206 MT   latt

28. 10:6a οὗτος ξενίζεται–𝔓⁷⁴ ℵ A B C E L P 049 105 206 322
               323 429 453 522 630 945 1175 1704 1739
               1891 2200 MT

     καὶ αὐτός ἐστιν ξενιζόμενος–614 d

29. 10:6b παρά τινι Σίμωνι Βυρσεῖ–𝔓⁷⁴ ℵ A B (C) E L P 049 81
               105 206 322 323 429 453 522 630 945 1175
               1704 1739 1891 2200 MT

     πρὸς Σίμωνα τινα Βυρσέα– 614

30. 10:6c omit–𝔓⁷⁴ ℵ A B C E L P 049 81 105 206 322 323 429
               453 522 614 630 945 1175 1704 1739 1891
               2200 MT it sa bo

     ὃς λαλήσει ῥήματα πρός σε ἐν οἷς σωθήσῃ σὺ καὶ πᾶς
     οἶκος σοῦ–(69ᵐᵍ) 913 1292 vgᶜˡ

31. 10:7 αὐτῷ–𝔓⁷⁴ℵ A B C E 81 322 323 429 453 522 (630) 945
             1175 1704 1739 1891 2200 it sa bo

     τῷ κορνηλίῳ–L P 049 105 206 614 MT

32. 10:10 ἐγένετο²–𝔓⁷⁴ ℵ A B C P 322 323 429 453 522 630 945
             1175 1704 1739 1891 2200 bo Or

     ἐπέπεσεν–E L 049 105 206 614 MT latt sy sa

     ἦλθεν–𝔓⁴⁵

33. 10:11 καὶ καταβαῖνον σκεῦός τι ὡς ὀθόνην μεγάλην
τέσσαρσιν ἀρχαῖς καθιέμενον–𝔓⁷⁴ ℵ A B C
E 1175 vg
καὶ καταβαῖνον σκεῦός τι ὡς ὀθόνην μεγάλην
τέσσαρσιν ἀρχαῖς δεδεμένον καὶ
καθιέμενον–81 322 323 429 453 522 630 945
1704 1739 1891 2200 (it sy)
καὶ καταβαῖνον ἐπ' αὐτὸν σκεῦός τι ὡς ὀθόνην μεγάλην
τέσσαρσιν ἀρχαῖς δεδεμένος καὶ
καθιέμενον–L P 049 105 206 614 MT
καὶ τέσσαρσιν ἀρχαῖς δεδεμένον σκεῦός τι ὡς ὀθόνην
μεγάλην καταβαῖνον καὶ καθιέμενον–Ψ
καὶ τέσσαρσιν ἀρχαῖς δεδεμένον σκεῦος τι καθιέμενον–
𝔓⁴⁵

34. 10:12 τὰ τετράποδα καὶ ἑρπετὰ τῆς γῆς–𝔓⁷⁴ ℵ A B 81 1175
lat sa bo Cl Or

τὰ τετράποδα καὶ τὰ ἑρπετὰ τῆς γῆς–429 522 630 945
1704 1739 1891 2200

τὰ τετράποδα τῆς γῆς καὶ τὰ θηρία καὶ τὰ ἑρπετὰ–L P
049 105 206 614 MT

τὰ τετράποδα καὶ τὰ θηρία καὶ τὰ ἑρπετὰ τῆς γῆς–Cᵛⁱᵈ
E 322 323 453

35. 10:16 εὐθὺς ἀνελήμφθη–𝔓⁷⁴ ℵ A B Cᵛⁱᵈ E 81 vg syʰᵐᵍ bo

πάλιν ἀνελήμφθη–(D) L P 049 105 206 322 323 429 522
614 630 945 1704 1739 1891 2200 MT syʰ
saᵐˢˢ mae

εὐθέως ἀνελήμφθη πάλιν–326

ἀνελήμφθη–453 1175 d syᵖ saᵐˢˢ boᵐˢˢ

36.   10:19   τρεῖς–𝔓⁷⁴ ℵ A B C E 81 322 323 429 453 522 630 945
           1175 1704 1739 1891   TR   lat syᵖ· ʰᵐᵍ sa bo

         δύο–B

         omit –D H L P 049 105 206 614 2200 MT   l p* syʰ   Spec
         Ambr Aug

37.   10:21   omit–𝔓⁴⁵ 𝔓⁷⁴ ℵ A B C D E L P 81 105 322 323 429 453
                 522 614   630 945 1175 1704 1739 1891 2200
                 MT sa bo

         τοὺς ἀπεσταλμένους ἀπὸ Κορνηλίου πρὸς αὐτόν–H (049)
         (206) TR w

38.   10:23   ἀναστὰς ἐξῆλθεν–𝔓⁷⁴ ℵ A B D 81 1175   sa bo

         ὁ Πέτρος ἐξῆλθεν–H L P 049 105 206 MT

         ἀναστὰς ὁ Πέτρος ἐξῆλθεν–C E 322 323 429 453 522 614
         630 945 1704 1739 1891 2200   gig

39.   10:25   ὡς δὲ ἐγένετο τοῦ εἰσελθεῖν συναντήσας αὐτῷ ὁ
            Κορνήλιος–𝔓⁷⁴ ℵ A B C E (H) L P (049) 81
            105 206 322 323 429 453 522 614   630 945
            1175 1704 1739 1891 2200   MT sa bo

         προσεγγίζοντες δὲ τοῦ Πέτρου εἰς τὴν Καισαρίαν
         προδραμὼν εἷς τῶν δούλων διεσάφησεν
         παραγεγονέναι αὐτὸν ὁ δὲ Κορνήλιος
         ἐκπηδήσας καὶ συναντήσας αὐτῷ– D   (gig
         syʰᵐᵍ mae)

40. 10:26 omit–𝔓⁵⁰ 𝔓⁷⁴ ℵ A B C H L P 049 81 105 206 322 323
429 453 522 614 630 945 1175 1704 1739
1891 2200 MT

ὡς καὶ σύ–D* E   it mae bo^mss

41. 10:29 omit–𝔓⁵⁰ 𝔓⁷⁴ ℵ A B C H L P 049 81 105 206 322 323
429 453 522 614 630 945 1175 1704 1739
1891 2200 MT

ὑφ' ὑμῶν–D E p

42. 10:30 τὴν ἐνάτην–𝔓⁷⁴ ℵ A B C 81 322 323 630 945 1704 1739
1891 2200* vg bo

νηστεύων καὶ τὴν ἐνάτην ὥραν–(𝔓⁵⁰) Aᶜ (D) H P 049 105
206 429 453 522 614 1175   MT sy sa mae

νηστεύων καὶ προσευχόμενος ἀπὸ ἐκτῆς ὥρας ἕως
ἐνάτης–E

43. 10:32 omit–𝔓⁴⁵ 𝔓⁷⁴ ℵ A B 81 453   vg bo

ὃς παραγενόμενος λαλήσει σοι– C D E H L P 049 105
206 322 323 429 522 614 630 945 1175 1704
1739 1891 2200 MT it sy (sa) (mae)

44. 10:33 omit–𝔓⁷⁴ ℵ A B C E H L P 049 81 105 206 322 323 429
453 522 614 630 945 1175 1704 1739 1891
2200   MT sa bo

παρακαλῶν ἐλθεῖν σε πρὸς ἡμᾶς–D p sy^{h**} mae

45.   10:41a omit–𝔓⁷⁴ ℵ A B C E H L P 049 81 105 206 322 323 429
                        453 522 614 630 945 1175 1704 1739 1891
                        2200 MT sa bo

       καὶ συνεστράφημεν–D   it syʰ mae

46.   10:41b omit–𝔓⁷⁴ ℵ A B C H L P 049 81 105 206 322 323 429
                        453 522 614 630 945 1175 1704 1739 1891
                        2200 MT bo

       δι' ἡμερῶν τεσσαράκοντα–(D) E   it sa mae

47.   10:48 ἐν τῷ ὀνόματι Ἰησοῦ Χριστοῦ βαπτισθῆναι–𝔓⁷⁴ ℵ A B
                        (81) 1175

       βαπτισθῆναι ἐν τῷ ὀνόματι Ἰησοῦ Χριστοῦ–E 322 323
                        429 453 614 945 1704 1739 1891 2200   sa bo

       βαπτισθῆναι ἐν τῷ ὀνόματι τοῦ κυρίου–(D) H L P 049
                        105 (206)   MT   vg p gig

48.   14:2a omit–𝔓⁷⁴ ℵ A B C E L P 049 81 105 206 322 323 429
                        453 522 614 630 945 1175 1704 1739 1891
                        2200   MT gig syʰ sa bo

       ἀρχισυνάγωγοι τῶν Ἰουδαίων καὶ οἱ ἄρχοντες τῆς
                        συναγωγῆς ἐπήγαγον αὐτοῖς διωγμὸν κατὰ
                        τῶν δικαίων–D (syʰᵐᵍ)

49.   14:2b omit–𝔓⁴⁵ 𝔓⁷⁴ ℵ A B C L P 049 81 105 206 322 323 429
                        453 522 630 945 1175 1704 1739 1891 2200
                        MT sa bo

       διωγμόν–(D) E 614   gig syʰ

50.   14:2c omit–𝔓⁷⁴ ℵ A B C L P 049 81 105 206 322 323 429 453
              522 614 630 945 1175 1704 1739 1891 2200
              MT sa bo

      ὁ δὲ κύριος ἔδωκεν ταχὺ εἰρήνην–D (E)   gig p w syʰᵐᵍ
      mae

51.   14:4 omit–𝔓⁷⁴ ℵ A B C E L P 049 81 105 206 322 323 429 453
              522 614 630 945 1175 1704 1739 1891 2200
              MT it sa bo

      κολλώμενοι διὰ τὸν λόγον τοῦ θεοῦ–D syʰᵐᵍ

52.   14:6 omit–𝔓⁷⁴ ℵ A B C D E L P 049 81 105 322 323 453 614
              630 945 1175 1704 1739 1891 2200   MT it
              sa bo

      οἱ ἀπόστολοι–206 429 522

53.   14:7 omit–𝔓⁷⁴ ℵ A B C H L P 049 81 105 206 322 323 429 453
              522 614 630 945 1175 1704 1739 1891 2200
              MT   sa bo

      καὶ ἐκινήθη ὅλον τὸ πλῆθος ἐπὶ τῇ διδαχῇ ὁ δὲ Παῦλος
      καὶ Βαρνάβας διέτριβον ἐν Λύστροις–D (E)
      h w vgˢ (mae)

54.   14:8 omit–ℵ A B C D E 81 453 614 1175 1739

      ὑπάρχων–H L P 049 105 322 323 1891   MT

      ὤν–206 429 522 630 945 1704 2200

55.   14:9 ὃς ἀτενίσας αὐτῷ–𝔓⁷⁴ ℵ A B C H L P 049 81 105 206
                322 323 429 453 522 614 630 945 1175 1704
                1739 1891 2200 MT sa bo

         ἀτενίσας δὲ αὐτῷ ὁ Παῦλος–D (E)   h

56.   14:10a omit–𝔓⁷⁴ ℵ A B H L P 049 81 105   MT gig vg syʰ boᵖᵗ

         σοὶ λέγω ἐν τῷ ὀνόματι τοῦ κυρίου'Ιησοῦ Χριστοῦ–C D
         (E) 206 322 323 (429) 453 522 614 630 945
         1175 1704 1739 1891 2200   h t syᵖˑʰᵐᵍ sa
         Irˡᵃᵗ

57.   14:10b omit–𝔓⁷⁴ ℵ A B C H L P 049 81 105 206 322 323 429
                453 522 614 630 945 1175 1704 1739 1891
                2200 MT sa bo

         εὐθέως παραχρῆμα–D (E)   syʰᵐᵍ mae

58.   14:14 ἀκούσαντες δὲ οἱ ἀπόστολοι–𝔓⁷⁴ ℵ A B C E H L P 049
                81 105 206 322 323 429 453 522 614 630 945
                1175 1704 1739 1891 2200 MT   sa bo

         ἀκούσας δέ–D   gig h syᵖ

59.   14:18 omit–𝔓⁷⁴ ℵ A B D E H L P 049 105 206 322 323 429 522
                945 1704 1739 1891 MT   sa bo

         ἀλλὰ πορεύεσθαι ἕκαστον εἰς τὰ ἴδια–C 81 453 614 630
         1175 2200 (h) syʰᵐᵍ

60.   14:19a ἐπῆλθον δέ–א A B H L P 105 614   MT   sa bo

.διατριβόντων δὲ αὐτῶν καὶ διδασκόντων ἐπῆλθον–C D E
81 206 322 323 429 453 522 630 945 1175
1704 1739 1891 2200   h sy^{hmg} mae

61.   14:19b καὶ πείσαντες τοὺς ὄχλους–𝔓⁷⁴ א A B D E H L P 049
105 614   MT   sa bo

καὶ διαλεγομένων αὐτῶν παρρησίᾳ ἔπεισαν τοὺς ὄχλους
ἀποστῆναι ἀπ' αὐτῶν λέγοντες ὅτι οὐδὲν
ἀληθὲς λέγουσιν ἀλλὰ πάντα ψεύδονται καὶ
πείσαντες τοὺς ὄχλους–C 81 206 322 323
(429) 453 522 630 945 1175 1704 1739 1891
2200   (h) sy^{hmg} mae

62.   14:25a omit–B D H L P 049 105 206 322 323 429 453 522 630
945 1175 1704 1739 1891 2200   MT sa

τοῦ κυρίου–א A C 81 614   vg sy^{p, h**}

τοῦ θεοῦ–𝔓⁷⁴ E   gig bo^{ms}

63.   14:25b omit–𝔓⁷⁴ א A B C E H L P 049 81 105 206 322 323 429
453 522 945 1175 1704 1739 1891 2200   MT
sa bo

εὐαγγελιζόμενοι αὐτούς–D 614   sy^{h**} mae

64.   15:1a   omit–𝔓⁷⁴ ℵ A B C D E H L P 049 81 105 206 322 323
                429 453 522 630 945 1175 1704 1739 1891
                2200 MT sa bo

      τῶν πεπιστευκότων ἀπὸ τῆς αἱρέσεως τῶν φαρισαίων–
      614 sy^hmg

65.   15:1b   τῷ ἔθει τῷ Μωϋσέως–𝔓⁷⁴ ℵ A B C E H L P 049 81 105
                206 322 323 (429) 453 522 614 630 945 1175
                1704 1739 1891 2200 MT it bo

      καὶ τῷ ἔθει Μωσέως περιπάτητε–D (sy^p) sa mae

66.   15:2a   ἔταξαν ἀναβαίνειν Παῦλον καὶ Βάρναβαν καί τινας
                ἄλλους ἐξ αὐτῶν–𝔓⁷⁴ ℵ A B C E H L P 049
                81 105 206 322 323 429 453 522 614 630 945
                1175 1704 1739 1891 2200 MT sa bo

      ἔλεγεν γὰρ ὁ Παῦλος μένειν οὕτως καθὼς ἐπίστευσαν
      διϊσχυριζόμενος οἱ δὲ ἐληλυθότες ἀπὸ
      Ἰερουσαλὴμ παρήγγειλαν αὐτοῖς τῷ Παύλῳ
      καὶ Βαρνάβᾳ καί τισιν ἄλλοις ἀναβαίνειν–
      D gig w sy^hmg mae

67.   15:2b   omit–𝔓⁷⁴ ℵ A B C E H L P 049 81 105 206 322 323 429
                453 522 630 945 1175 1704 1739 1891 2200
                MT sa bo

      ὅπως κριθῶσιν ἐπ᾽ αὐτοῖς–D (614) sy^h**

68. 15:4a omit–𝔓⁷⁴ ℵ A B E H L P 049 81 105 206 322 323 429
    453 522 630 945 1175 1704 1739 1891 2200
    MT bo

    μεγάλως–C (D) 614   syʰ** sa

69. 15:4b omit–𝔓⁷⁴ ℵ A B C D E P 049 81 105 322 323 453 1175
    1739 1891 MT it sa bo

    καὶ ὅτι ἤνοιξεν τοῖς ἔθνεσι θύραν πίστεως–H L 206 429
    522 614 630 945 1704 2200

70. 15:6a omit–𝔓⁷⁴ ℵ A B C D E H L P 049 81 105 206 322 323
    429 453 522 630 945 1175 1704 1739 1891
    2200 MT sa bo

    σὺν τῷ πλήθει–614 syʰ

71. 15:6b λόγου–𝔓⁷⁴ ℵ A B C D H L P 049 81 105 206 322 323
    429 453 522 630 945 1175 1704 1739 1891
    2200 MT sa bo

    ζητήματος–E 614   gig syʰ

72. 15:7 ἀρχαίων ἐν ὑμῖν ἐξελέξατο ὁ θεός–𝔓⁷⁴ ℵ A B C 81 (206)
    429 453 (522) 630 945 1175 1704 1739 1891
    2200

    ἀρχαίων ὁ θεὸς ἐν ἡμῖν ἐξελέξατο–E H L P 049 105 MT

    ἀρχαίων ἐν ἡμῖν ὁ θεὸς ἐξελέξατο–(D) 322 323 (614)
    gig Ir Amb

    ἀρχαίων ὁ θεὸς ἐξελέξατο–69

73.　15:10　οἱ πατέρες ἡμῶν οὔτε ἡμεῖς–𝔓⁷⁴ ℵ A B C D E H L P
049 81 105 206 322 323 429 453 522 630 945
1175 1704 1739 1891 2200 MT

ἡμεῖς οὔτε οἱ πατέρες ἡμῶν–614 Tert

74.　15:18　γνωστὰ ἀπ' αἰῶνος–ℵ B C 81 (206) 322 323 (429) (522)
630 (945) 1175 (1704) 1739 1891 2200 sa bo

γνωστὰ ἀπ' αἰῶνός ἐστι τῷ θεῷ πάντα τὰ ἔργα αὐτοῦ–E
H L P 049 105 614 MT lat (sy) Ir

γνωστὸν ἀπ' αἰῶνος τῷ κυρίῳ τὸ ἔργον αὐτοῦ–𝔓⁷⁴ A (D)

75.　15:20a　καὶ τῆς πορνείας καὶ τοῦ πνικτοῦ καὶ τοῦ αἵματος–
(𝔓⁷⁴) ℵ (A) (B) Cⱽⁱᵈ E H L P 049 (81) 105 322
323 453 614　MT sa bo

καὶ τοῦ αἵματος καὶ τοῦ πνικτοῦ καὶ τῆς πορνείας–206
429 522 630 945 1704 1739 1891 2200

καὶ τοῦ πνικτοῦ καὶ τοῦ αἵματος–𝔓⁴⁵

καὶ τῆς πορνείας καὶ τοῦ αἵματος–D gig Ir

76.　15:20b　omit–𝔓⁷⁴ ℵ A B C E H L P 049 81 105 453 614 1175
MT bo

καὶ ὅσα ἂν μὴ θέλωσιν ἑαυτοῖς γίνεσθαι ἕτερος μὴ
ποιεῖν–D 206 322 323 429 522 630 945 1704
1739 1891 2200 sa Irˡᵃᵗ

77.   15:21 κατὰ πόλιν τοὺς κηρύσσοντας αὐτόν–𝔭⁷⁴ ℵ A B D E H
L P 049 81 105 206 322 323 429 453 522 614
630 945 1704 1739 1891 2200   MT

τοὺς κηρύσσοντας αὐτὸν κατὰ πόλιν–C 1175

τοὺς κηρύσσοντας αὐτόν–𝔭⁴⁵

78.   15:23 διὰ χείρος αὐτῶν (τάδε)–𝔭⁷⁴ ℵ A B E H L P 049 81 105
206 322 323 429 453 522 630 945 1175 1704
1739 1891 2200 MT syʰ bo

διὰ χείρος αὐτῶν ἐπιστόλην καὶ πέμψαντες
περιέχουσαν τάδε–(C) (D) 614 gig w (syᵖ)
(sa)

79.   15:24a ἐξελθόντες–𝔭⁷⁴ A C D E (H) (L) P 049 81 105 322 323
429 522 614 630 945 1704 1739 1891 2200
MT latt sy (sa) bo Irˡᵃᵗ

omit–ℵ* B 206 1175

80.   15:24b omit–𝔭⁷⁴ ℵ A B D 81 (1175)   vg sa bo

λέγοντες περιτέμνεσθαι καὶ τηρεῖν τὸν νόμον–C E H L
P 049 105 206 322 323 429 453 522 614 630
945 1704 1739 1891 2200   MT (gig) sy

81.   15:26 omit–𝔭⁷⁴ ℵ A B C H L P 049 33 81 105 206 322 323 429
453 522 630 945 1175 1704 1739 1891 2200
MT sa bo

εἰς πάντα πειρασμόν–D E 614 l syʰᵐᵍ

82. 15:29 omit–𝔓⁷⁴ ℵ A B C E H L P 049 81 105 453 1175   MT
bo

καὶ ὅσα μὴ θέλετε ἑαυτοῖς γίνεσθαι ἑτέροις μὴ ποιεῖν–
D 206 322 323 429 522 614 630 945 1704
1739 1891 2200 l p w syʰ** sa   Ir Cyp

83. 15:33 ἀποστείλαντες αὐτούς–𝔓⁷⁴ ℵ A B C D 81 206 322 323
429 453 522 630 945 1175 1704 1739 1891
2200   sa bo

ἀποστόλους–E H L P 049 105 614 MT

84. 15:34 omit–𝔓⁷⁴ ℵ A B E H L P 049 81 105 MT   vgˢᵗ syᵖ bo

ἔδοξε δὲ τῷ Σιλᾷ ἐπιμεῖναι αὐτοῦ–C (D) 206 322 323
(429) 453 522 614 630 1175 1704 1739 1891
2200   TR syʰ** sa boᵐˢˢ (gig) (l) (w)
(vgᶜˡ)

85. 15:41 omit–𝔓⁷⁴ ℵ A B C E H L P 049 81 105 206 322 323 429
453 522 614 630 945 1175 1704 1739 1891
2200 MT sa bo

παραδιδοὺς τὰς ἐντολὰς τῶν πρεσβυτέρων–D gig w vgᶜˡ
syʰᵐᵍ

86. 18:4 διελέγετο δὲ ἐν τῇ συναγωγῇ κατὰ πᾶν σάββατον ἔπειθέν τε Ἰουδαίους καὶ Ἕλληνας–𝔓⁷⁴ ℵ A B E H L P 049 105 206 322 323 429 453 522 614 630 945 1175 1704 1739 1891 2200 MT sa bo

εἰσπορευόμενος δὲ εἰς τὴν συναγωγὴν κατὰ πᾶν σάββατον διελέγετο καὶ ἐντιθεὶς τὸ ὄνομα τοῦ κυρίου Ἰησοῦ καὶ ἔπειθεν δὲ οὐ μόνον Ἰουδαίους ἀλλὰ καὶ Ἕλληνας–D h (gig) (syʰᵐᵍ)

87. 18:5a λόγῳ–𝔓⁷⁴ ℵ A B D E 614   lat sy sa bo   Thdrt

πνεύματι–H L P 049 105 206 322 323 429 453 522 630 945 1175 1704 1739 1891 2200 MT   syʰᵐᵍ

88. 18:5b εἶναι–𝔓⁷⁴ ℵ A B D 206 322 323 453 522 630 945 1175 1704 1739 1891 2200

omit–E H L P 049 105 429 614 MT

89. 18:6 omit–𝔓⁷⁴ ℵ A B E H L P 049 105 206 322 323 429 453 522 614 630 945 1175 1704 1739 1891 2200 MT sa bo

πολλοῦ δὲ λόγου γινομένου καὶ γραφῶν διερμηνευομένων–D h (syʰᵐᵍ)

90. 18:7a omit–𝔓⁷⁴ ℵ A B E H L P 049 105 206 322 323 429 453 522 630 945 1175 1704 1739 1891 2200 MT sa bo

ἀπὸ τοῦ Ἀκύλα–D* 614 (h)

91.   18:7b Τιτίου 'Ιούστου–𝔓⁷⁴ ℵ B E P 453 630 945 1175 1704
         1739 1891 2200 gig

       'Ιούστου–A D H L 049 105 206 322 323 429 522 614   MT
       h p

       Τίτος–sa bo

       omit–325

92.   18:8 omit–𝔓⁷⁴ ℵ A B E H L P 049 105 206 322 323 429 453
                522 630 945 1175 1704 1739 1891 2200 MT
                sa bo

       διὰ τοῦ ὀνόματος τοῦ κυρίου 'Ιησοῦ Χριστοῦ–D 614
       syʰ** h

93.   18:9 ἐν νυκτὶ δι' ὁράματος–𝔓⁷⁴ ℵ B 206 429 453 522 630 945
                1175 1704 1739 1891 2200

       δι' ὁράματος ἐν νυκτί–(D) E (H) L P 049 105 322 323
                614 MT gig

       ἐν ὁράματι–A h syᵖ

94.   18:12 τῷ Παύλῳ καί–𝔓⁷⁴ ℵ A B E H L P 049 105 206 322 323
                429 453 522 614 630 945 1175 1704 1739
                1891 2200 MT bo

       συλλαλήσαντες μεθ' ἑαυτῶν ἐπὶ τὸν Παῦλον καὶ
       ἐπιθέντες τὰς χεῖρας - D   h (syʰ**) (sa)

95. 18:17 omit–𝔓⁷⁴ ℵ A B   vg bo

οἱ "Ελληνες–D E H L P 049 105 206 322 323 429 522 614
630 945 1175 1704 1739 1891 2200   MT
gig h sy sa

οἱ ᾽Ιουδαῖοι–453

96. 18:18 ἐν Κεχρεαῖς τὴν κεφάλην–𝔓⁷⁴ ℵ A B 206 429 453 522
630 945 1175 1704 1739 1891 2200

τὴν κεφάλην ἐν Κεχρεαῖς–D E H L P 049 105 322 323
614   MT

97. 18:19 κἀκείνους κατέλιπεν αὐτοῦ–𝔓⁷⁴ ℵ A B E H L P 049 105
206 322 323 429 453 522 630 945 1175 1704
1739 1891 2200   MT

καὶ τῷ εἰπόντι σαββάτῳ ἐκείνους κατέλιπεν ἐκεῖ–D
(614) (h) (shʰ**)

98. 18:20 μεῖναι–𝔓⁷⁴ ℵ A B 453 945 1175 1704 1739 1891

μεῖναι παρ᾽ αὐτοῖς–D E H L P 049 105 206 322 323 429
522 614 630 2200   MT   w sy sa bo

99. 18:21a ἀποταξάμενος καί–𝔓⁷⁴ ℵ A B D

ἀπετάξατο αὐτοῖς–H L P 049 105 322 323 614 2200
MT

ἀποταξάμενος αὐτοῖς καί–E 206 429 453 522 630 945
1175 1704 1739 1891

100.   18:21b omit–𝔓⁷⁴ ℵ A B E 206 429 453 522 945 1704 1739 1891
       2200 sa bo

       δεῖ με πάντως τὴν ἑορτὴν τὴν ἐρχομένην ποιῆσαι εἰς
           Ἱεροσόλυμα–D H L P 049 105 322 323 614
       630 1175 MT gig w sy

101.   18:21/2 ἀνήχθη ἀπὸ τῆς Ἐφέσου καὶ κατελθών–𝔓⁷⁴ ℵ A B D E
              H L P 049 105 206 322 323 429 453 522 630
              945 1175 1704 1739 1891 2200 MT sa bo

       καὶ ἀνήχθη ἀπὸ τῆς Ἐφέσου τὸν δὲ Ἀκύλαν εἴασεν ἐν
           Ἐφέσῳ· αὐτὸς δὲ ἀνηχθεὶς ἦλθες–614
       syp.hmg

102.   18:25 τὴν ὁδόν–𝔓⁷⁴ ℵ A B E H L P 049 105 614 1175 MT sa
       bo

       τὸν λόγον–(D) 206 322 323 429 453 522 630 945 1704
           1739 1891 2200 (gig)

103.   18:26 τὴν ὁδὸν τοῦ θεοῦ–𝔓⁷⁴ ℵ A B (D) (E) (H) (L) (P) (049)
              (105) 206 453 614 1175 (MT) (vgcl) (syp)

       τὸν λόγον τοῦ κυρίου–322 323 945 1704 1739 1891 2200

       τὸν λόγον τοῦ θεοῦ–429 522 630

104. 18:27 βουλομένου δὲ αὐτοῦ διελθεῖν εἰς τὴν Ἀχαΐαν
προτρεψάμενοι οἱ ἀδελφοὶ ἔγραψεν τοῖς
μαθηταῖς ἀποδέξασθαι αὐτόν· ὃς
παραγενόμενος συνεβάλετο–𝔓⁷⁴ ℵ A B E H
L P 049 105 206 322 323 429 453 522 614
630 945 1175 1704 1739 1891 2200 MT it
sa bo

ἐν δὲ τῇ Ἐφέσῳ ἐπιδημοῦντές τινες Κορίνθιοι καὶ
ἀκούσαντες αὐτοῦ παρεκάλουν διελθεῖν σὺν
αὐτοῖς εἰς τὴν πατρίδα αὐτῶν
συγκατανεύασντος δὲ αὐτοῦ οἱ Ἐφέσιοι
ἔγραψαν τοῖς ἐν Κορίνθῳ μαθηταῖς ὅπως
ἀποδέξωνται τὸν ἄνδρα ὃς ἐπιδημήσας εἰς
τὴν Ἀχαΐαν πολὺ συνεβάλλετο ἐν ταῖς
ἐκκλησίαις–𝔓³⁸ D (syʰᵐᵍ)

105. 18:27b διὰ τῆς χάριτος–𝔓⁷⁴ ℵ A B E H L P 049 105 206 322
323 429 453 522 630 945 1175 1704 1739
1891 2200 MT sa bo

omit–614

106. 18:28 omit–𝔓⁷⁴ ℵ A B H L P 049 105 206 322 323 429 453 522
630 945 1175 1704 1739 1891 2200 MT sa
bo

διαλεγόμενος καί–𝔓³⁸ D 614

καὶ κατ᾽ οἶκον–E

107.　20:1a μεταπεμψάμενος–𝔓⁷⁴ ℵ B E 453 1175

　　　μεταστειλάμενος–206 429 630 945 1704 1739 1891 2200

　　　προσκαλεσάμενος–A D H L P 049 105 322 323 614　MT
　　　latt sy

108.　20:1b παρακαλέσας–𝔓⁷⁴ ℵ A B D E 206 322 323 429 453 614
　　　　　　630 945 1175 1704 1739 1891 2200　it sa bo

　　　omit–H L P 049 105　MT

109.　20:1c πορεύεσθαι εἰς Μακεδονίαν–𝔓⁷⁴ ℵ (A) B (H) (L) (P)
　　　　　　(049) (105) 206 (429) 453 (614) (630) 1175
　　　　　　(1891) (2200) (MT)　sa bo

　　　εἰς Μακεδονίαν–D E 322 (323) 945 1704 1739　gig
　　　bomss

110.　20:3 μέλλοντι ἀνάγεσθαι εἰς τὴν Συρίαν ἐγένετο γνώμης
　　　　　　τοῦ–𝔓⁷⁴ ℵ A B E H L P 049 105 206 322 323
　　　　　　(429) 453 522 614 630 945 1175 1704 1739
　　　　　　1891 2200　MT sa bo

　　　ἠθέλησεν ἀναχθῆναι εἰς Συρίαν εἶπεν δὲ τὸ πνεῦμα αὐτῷ
　　　- D (gig) syhmg

111. 20:4a συνείπετο δὲ αὐτῷ–𝔓⁷⁴ ℵ B

συνείπετο δὲ αὐτῷ ἄχρι τῆς ᾿Ασίας–A E H L P 049 105
206 322 323 429 453 522 614 630 945 (1175)
1704 1739 1891 2200 MT gig vg^mss sy sa

μέλλοντος οὖν ἐξειέναι αὐτοῦ μέχρι τῆς ᾿Ασίας–D
(sy^hmg)

112. 20:4b Πύρρου–𝔓⁷⁴ ℵ A B D E 206 322 323 429 453 522 630 945
1175 1704 1739 1891 2200 latt sy^hmg sa bo

oimt–H L P 049 105 614 MT sy

113. 20:7 ἡμῶν–𝔓⁷⁴ ℵ A B D E 429* 453 522 614 630 945 1175
1704 1739 1891 2200 sa bo

τῶν μαθητῶν–H L P 049 105 322 323 429^c MT

αὐτῶν–206

114. 20:15 τῇ δέ–𝔓⁷⁴ ℵ A B C E 206 429 453 630 1175 1739 1891
2200 vg bo

καὶ μείναντες ἐν Τρωγυλλίῳ τῇ - D H L P 049 105 322
323 614 (945) 1704 MT gig sy sa

115. 20:16a ὅπως μὴ γένηται αὐτῷ χρονοτρίβησαι–𝔓⁷⁴ ℵ A B C E
H L P 049 105 206 322 323 429 453 522 614
630 945 1175 1704 1739 1891 2200   MT sa
bo

μήποτε γενήθη αὐτῷ κατάσχεσίς τις - D (gig) vg

116.　20:16b εἰ δυνατὸν εἴη αὐτῷ–𝔓⁷⁴ ℵ A B C E 206 322 323 429
　　　　　　　　522 630 945 1175 1704 1739 1891 2200　it sa
　　　　　　　　bo

　　　εἰ δυνατὸν ἦν αὐτῷ–L P 049 105 614　MT

　　　omit–D H

117.　20:18　omit–ℵ B C H L P 049 105 206 322 323 429 453 522 614
　　　　　　　　630 945 1175 1704 1739 1891　MT

　　　ὁμόσε ὄντων αὐτῶν–𝔓⁷⁴ A (D) E　lat

118.　20:19a　omit–𝔓⁷⁴ ℵ A B D E H L P 049 105 206 322 323 429
　　　　　　　　522 630 945 1175 1704 1739 1891　MT

　　　μεθ' ὑμῶν–C 453 614

119.　20:19b omit–𝔓⁷⁴ ℵ A B D E　sa bo

　　　πολλῶν–C H L P 049 105 206 322 323 429 453 522 614
　　　　　　　　630 945 (1175) 1704 1739 1891　MT

120.　20:23　μένουσιν–𝔓⁷⁴ ℵ A B C E H L P 049 206 322 323 429
　　　　　　　　453 522 630 945 1175 1704 1739 1891　MT
　　　　　　　　bo

　　　μένουσίν μοι ἐν 'Ιερουσαλήμ–D (614) (gig) (vgᶜˡ) (syʰ**)
　　　　　　　　sa

121.   20:24a λόγου ποιοῦμαι–ℵ* B C 1175   (gig) (sy^p)

       λόγον ἔχω οὐδὲ ποιοῦμαι–𝔓⁷⁴ ℵ^c A (D)

       λόγον ποιοῦμαι οὐδὲ ἔχω–E H L P 049 206 322 323 429
           453 522 614 630 945 1704 1739 1891   MT
           (sy^h)

122.   20:24b omit–𝔓⁷⁴ ℵ A B D   lat sy^p sa bo

       μετὰ χαρᾶς–C E H L P 049 206 322 323 429 453 522 614
           630 945 1175 1704 1739 1891   MT   sy^h

123.   20:24c omit–𝔓⁷⁴ ℵ A B C E H L P 049 206 322 323 429 453
           522 614 630 945 1175 1704 1739 1891   MT
           bo

       Ἰουδαίοις καὶ Ἕλλησιν–𝔓⁴¹ D   gig sa^mss   Lcf

124.   20:25a τὴν βασιλείαν–𝔓⁷⁴ ℵ A B C D E H L P 049 453 614
           1175   MT   it sa bo

       τὸ εὐαγγέλιον–206 322 323 429 522 630 945 1704 1739
           1891

125.   20:25b omit–𝔓⁷⁴ ℵ A B C 453   sy bo^pt

       τοῦ θεοῦ–E H L P 049 206 322 323 429 522 614 630 945
           1175 1704 1739 1891   MT   vg bo^pt

       τοῦ Ἰησοῦ–D   sa

       domini iesu–gig   Lcif

126. 20:27 πάσαν τὴν βούλην τοῦ θεοῦ ὑμῖν–𝔓⁷⁴ ℵ B C D 323 453
            ·1175

        ὑμῖν πάσαν τὴν βούλην τοῦ θεοῦ–A E H L P 049 206 322
            429 522 614 630 945 1704 1739 1891   MT
            Ir

127. 20:28a θεοῦ–ℵ B 614 1175 1704 TR   vg sy boᵐˢ Cyr

        κυρίου–𝔓⁷⁴ A C D E 206 429 453 522 630 945 1739 1891
            gig p syʰᵐᵍ sa bo   Irˡᵃᵗ Lcf

        κυρίου καὶ θεοῦ–C³ H L P 049 322 323   MT

128. 20:28b αἵματος τοῦ ἰδίου–𝔓⁷⁴ ℵ A B C D E 206 429 453 522
            630 945 1175 (1704) 1739 1891   Cyr

        ἰδίου αἵματος–H L P 049 322 323 614   MT

129. 20:32a omit–𝔓⁷⁴ ℵ A B D 1175   it sa bo

        ἀδελφοί–C E H L P 049 105 206 322 323 429 453 522 614
            630 945 1704 1739 1891   MT

130. 20:32b omit–𝔓⁷⁴ ℵ A B C D E H L P 049 105 206 322 323 429
            453 522 630 945 1175 1704 1739 1891   MT
            it sa bo

        αὐτῷ ἡ δόξα εἰς τοὺς αἰῶνας ἀμήν–614 syʰ**

131. 20:37 ἱκανὸς δὲ κλαυθμὸς ἐγένετο πάντων–𝔓⁷⁴ (ℵ) A B C D
      E 206 429 453 522 630 945 1175 1704 1739
      1891

      ἱκανὸς δὲ ἐγένετο κλαυθμὸς πάντων–H L P 049 105 322
      323 MT

      ἐγένετο δὲ κλαυθμὸς ἱκανὸς πάντων–614

132. 24:1 πρεσβυτέρων τινῶν–𝔓⁷⁴ ℵ A B E 81 322 323 614 630 945
      1175 1739 1891 2200

      τῶν πρεσβυτέρων–H L P 049 105 206 429 453 522 1704
      MT syᵖ

133. 24:6-8 omit–𝔓⁷⁴ ℵ A B H L P 049 81 105 1175   MT   p* s vgˢᵗ
      sa bo

      καὶ κατὰ τὸν ἡμέτερον νόμον ἠθελήσαμεν κρίναι
      παρελθὼν δὲ Λυσίας ὁ χιλίαρχος μετὰ
      πολλῆς βίας ἐκ τῶν χειρῶν ἡμῶν ἀπήγαγε
      κελεύσας τοὺς κατηγόρους αὐτοῦ ἔρχεσθαι
      ἐπί σε–E 206 322 323 429 453 522 614 630
      945 1704 1739 1891 2200 TR gig vgᶜˡ sy⁽ᵖ⁾

134. 24:9 omit–𝔓⁷⁴ ℵ A B E H L P 049 81 105 206 322 323 429 453
      522 630 945 1175 1704 1739 1891 2200 MT
      it sa bo

      εἰπόντος δὲ αὐτοῦ ταῦτα–614 syʰ**

135. 24:10 omit–𝔭⁷⁴ ℵ A B H L P 049 81 105 206 429 522   MT

δίκαιον–E 322 323 453 614 630 945 1175 1704 1739
1891 2200   syʰ

136. 24:15 omit–𝔭⁷⁴ ℵ A B C 81 945 1175 1704 1739 1891   lat sa
bo

νεκρῶν–E H L P 049 105 206 322 323 429 453 522 614
630 2200   MT sy

137. 24:16 διὰ πάντος post ἄνθρωπος–𝔭⁷⁴ ℵ A B C H L P 049 81
105 206 322 323 429 453 522 630 945 1175
1704 1739 1891 2200   MT bo

διὰ πάντος ante πρός–E 614   gig sa

138. 24:17 ἐλεημοσύνας ποιήσων εἰς τὸ ἔθνος μου παρεγενόμην
καὶ προσφοράς–𝔭⁷⁴ ℵ* (A) B C 81 453 630
945 1175 1704 1739 1891 2200

ἐλεημοσύνας ποιήσων εἰς τὸ ἔθνος μου καὶ προσφορὰς
παρεγενόμην–ℵᶜ E 614

παρεγενόμην ἐλεημοσύνας ποιήσων εἰς τὸ ἔθνος μου καὶ
προσφοράς–H L P 049 105 206 322 323 429
522   MT

139. 24:19 ἀπὸ τῆς ᾿Ασίας ᾿Ιουδαῖοι–𝔭⁷⁴ ℵ A B H L P 049 81 105
206 429 522 2200   MT

τῶν ἀπὸ τῆς ᾿Ασίας ᾿Ιουδαίων–E 453 614 945

τῶν ἀπὸ τῆς ᾿Ασίας ᾿Ιουδαῖοι–C 322 323 630 1175 1704
1739 1891

140. 24:20 ἀδίκημα–𝔭⁷⁴ ℵ A B 81 1175 sa

ἐν ἐμοὶ ἀδίκημα–C E H L P 049 105 206 322 323 429 453
522 614 MT latt sy bo

ἀδίκημα ἐν ἐμοί–630 945 1704 1739 1891 2200

141. 24:22 ἀνεβάλετο δὲ αὐτοὺς ὁ Φῆλιξ–𝔭⁷⁴ ℵ A B C E 81 630 945
1175 1704 1739 1891 2200 latt sy bo

ἀκούσας δὲ ταῦτα ὁ Φῆλιξ ἀνεβάλετο αὐτούς–H L P 049
105 206 322 323 429 453 522 614 MT sa

142. 24:22 διαγνώσομαι–𝔭⁷⁴ ℵ A B C E H L P 049 81 105 206 429
453 522 614 1175 MT it sa bo

ἀκριβέστερον διαγνώσομαι–322 323 630 945 1704 1739
1891 2200

143. 24:23a αὐτόν–𝔭⁷⁴ ℵ A B E 81 614 630 945 1175 1704 1739
1891 2200 it bo

τὸν Παῦλον–H L P 049 105 206 322 323 429 453 MT sa

144. 24:23b omit–𝔭⁷⁴ ℵ A B C E 81 630 945 1175 1704 1739 1891
2200 latt sy bo

ἢ προσέρχεσθαι–H L P 049 105 (206) 322 323 429 453
522 614 MT sa

145.   24:25 κρίματος τοῦ μέλλοντος–𝔓⁷⁴ ℵ A B E 81 322 323 614
630 945 1704 1739 1891 2200

κρίματος τοῦ μέλλοντος ἔσεσθαι–H L P 049 105 206 429
522 MT

μέλλοντος κρίματος–C 453 1175

146.   24:26 omit–ℵ A B C E 33 81 945 1175 1739 1891   latt sy

ὅπως λύσῃ αὐτόν–H L P 049 105 (206) 322 323 (429) 453
(522) 614 (630) (1704) (2200)   MT   sa bo

147.   24:27 omit–𝔓⁷⁴ ℵ A B C E H L P 049 81 105 206 322 323 429
453 522 630 945 1175 1704 1739 1891 2200
MT   it sa bo

τὸν δὲ Παῦλον εἴασεν ἐν τηρήσει διὰ Δρούσιλλαν–614
sy[hmg]

The numbers of each kind of reading among the genetically significant variations for each manuscript are presented in Appendix I. A summary of those tables put into percentages is given below.

Table 12 shows the number of places in which each manuscript of the study supported a reading that had any significant level of support from the Egyptian textual tradition. In this category, 1739 and 1891 stand closer to the Egyptian tradition than the others. They are followed, fairly closely, by 945 2200 453 1704 and 630. There is then a break before the next level, consisting of 522 429 323 206 and 322.

When looking at the places in which the manuscripts support a reading that is clearly Egyptian (Table 13), seven of the manuscripts are fairly closely grouped together (1739 1891 945 1704 2200 453 and 630) and the other five fall significantly lower (522 429 323 206 and 322). This is the same division among the twelve that was observed in the first chart.

Table 12

MS	Some Egyptian
1739	79.5%
1891	79.4%
945	77.1%
2200	76.3%
453	76.2%
1704	75.9%
630	74.6%
522	70.2%
429	69.2%
323	64.7%
206	63.0%
322	62.3%

Table 13

MS	Clearly Egyptian
1739	53.6%
1891	52.7%
945	50.9%
1704	50.0%
2200	47.8%
453	45.3%
630	44.4%
522	32.7%
429	29.1%
323	23.2%
206	21.4%
322	21.4%

In examining those places at which a reading is supported by any significant level by the Byzantine textual tradition (Table 14), five manuscripts are grouped near the top, 206 322 323 429 and 522.

Table 14

MS	Some Byzantine
206	83.3%
322	80.4%
323	78.7%
429	78.2%
522	77.9%
453	72.3%
630	71.5%
2200	71.2%
1704	67.7%
945	67.2%
1739	64.4%
1891	64.2%

There is then a drop of 7.6% to three others, 453 630 and 2200, and then 1704 945 1739 and 1891 are at the bottom. It is no surprise that the four at the top of this chart are the four that were at the bottom of the two previous charts.

Table 15

MS	Clearly Byzantine
206	71.4%
322	59.2%
429	56.3%
522	53.2%
323	53.1%
453	46.8%
630	36.7%
2200	33.3%
1704	32.6%
945	30.6%
1891	27.1%
1739	26.5%

When looking at the percentage of time these manuscripts support readings that are clearly Byzantine (Table 15), there are again five manuscripts at the top, significantly higher than the rest (206 322 429 522 and 323). Codex 453 falls into the middle area, while 630 2200 1704 945 1891 and 1739 are significantly lower, and again 1891 and 1739 are lower than 945.

Table 16

MS	Some "Western"
323	22.7%
322	22.5%
1739	18.9%
1891	18.3%
1704	18.0%
2200	17.9%
945	17.6%
630	16.9%
206	16.7%
429	15.8%
522	15.3%
453	13.8%

Thus the examination of the genetically significant variations confirms that manuscripts 206 322 323 429 and 522 belong to the Byzantine textual tradition in Acts and that manuscripts 453 945 1704 1739 and 1891 are members of the Egyptian textual tradition. While manuscripts 630 1704 and 2200 appeared to be closer to the Byzantine tradition in the overall quantitative analysis, the genetically significant variations have demonstrated that they are, in fact, more closely aligned with the Egyptian.

It should also be noted here that none of the manuscripts involved shared a significant level of "Western" readings. This is true even after versions from the apparatus of NA[26] have been included in the examination. Though this includes the versions only in a representative way, nothing in that representation that would lead one to conclude that these manuscripts have been influenced in any significant way by that textual tradition. The figures are presented in Tables 16 and 17.

Based only on percentages, none of the ten manuscripts has been influenced significantly by the "Western" tradition. There is very little difference between the percentages in Table 17 and in Table 16 simply because most of the time that the manuscripts support a "Western" reading, they support a "clearly Western" reading. And, of course, the number of total readings for Table 17 is much smaller than for Table 16.

Table 17

MS	Clearly "Western"
322	17.1%
323	17.1%
1704	15.7%
1739	15.7%
1891	15.2%
945	14.5%
2200	14.3%
429	13.0%
522	13.0%
630	13.0%
206	11.6%
453	11.6%

In summary, the profiles generated from the genetically significant variations demonstrate that none of the twelve has been heavily influenced by the "Western" textual tradition in Acts. The profiles have shown conclusively that five of the manuscripts are more closely related to the Byzantine tradition (206 322 323 429 and 522) and seven are more closely related to the Egyptian tradition (453 630 945 1704 1739 1891 and 2200). Despite the differences in basic textual affinities, these twelve manuscripts exhibit a high level of agreement among themselves. The next chapter demonstrates and explores those relationships.

CHAPTER TWO

FAMILY 1739

After establishing as precisely as possible the textual affinities of the twelve manuscripts, it is now possible to investigate the familial relationships among them. In Tables 17–25, I present different sections of Acts and show how the manuscripts relate to each other for each (the sections being chapters 1–28, 1–14, 15–28, 1–6, 7–10, 11–14, 15–19, 20–24, 25–28). This allows one to see how the manuscripts relate in the whole book, in the two halves, and in different portions of Acts. Following these nine tables, twelve other tables are presented in which the information for all the sections is shown for each manuscript. First, I present the information for the different sections of Acts.

How the Manuscripts Compare Within Each Section of Acts

Table 18 demonstrates that these manuscripts agree among themselves for the entire book of Acts from a low of 71.4% (206 and 453) to a high of 93.0% (1739 and 1891). Manuscripts 206 and 453 are the only ones that fail to exceed 90% with at least one other manuscript while Codex 453 even fails to reach 80%. Also, The column under manuscript 453 is distinctive in that there is a spread of only 5.4% (from 71.4% to 76.6%). The smallest spread among the others is 16.1% (under 2200). This indicates the very mixed nature of 453 that will be discussed later. Codices 1891 and 945 are the only

Table 18
ACTS 1–28

206		322		323	
429	87.7	323	92.1	322	92.1
522	85.8	206	78.9	1704	77.9
630	80.8	429	78.2	429	77.8
2200	80.8	1704	78.1	1739	76.9
1704	79.7	2200	76.5	1891	76.9
1891	79.3	522	76.1	206	76.5
322	78.9	630	75.7	630	76.2
945	77.0	1891	74.4	945	76.0
323	76.5	1739	74.0	522	75.8
1739	76.2	945	73.3	2200	75.7
453	71.4	453	71.8	453	72.9
429		**453**		**522**	
522	91.1	1891	76.6	429	91.1
206	87.7	1739	75.7	206	85.8
630	85.1	2200	75.6	630	83.6
2200	84.2	630	74.8	2200	81.9
1891	83.7	945	73.8	1891	81.6
1704	82.5	429	73.6	1704	80.8
945	81.2	323	72.9	945	79.5
1739	80.8	1704	72.5	1739	79.1
322	78.2	522	72.1	322	76.1
323	77.8	322	71.8	323	75.8
453	73.6	206	71.4	453	72.1
630		**945**		**1704**	
2200	91.7	1739	92.7	945	91.0
1891	90.4	1704	91.0	1891	86.9
1739	87.0	1891	90.5	1739	85.6
945	86.1	630	86.1	630	84.4
429	85.1	2200	84.6	2200	84.4
1704	84.4	429	81.2	429	82.5
522	83.6	522	79.5	522	80.8
206	80.8	323	76.0	206	79.7
323	76.2	206	77.0	322	78.1
322	75.7	453	73.8	323	77.9
453	74.8	322	73.3	453	72.5
1739		**1891**		**2200**	
1891	93.0	1739	93.0	630	91.7
945	92.7	945	90.5	1891	88.9
630	87.0	630	90.4	1739	85.7
2200	85.7	2200	88.9	945	84.6
1704	85.6	1704	86.9	1704	84.4
429	80.8	429	83.7	429	84.2
522	79.1	522	81.6	522	81.9
323	76.9	206	79.3	206	80.8
206	76.2	323	76.9	322	76.5
453	75.7	453	76.6	323	75.7
322	74.0	322	74.4	453	75.6

ones to agree over 90% with three others. The manuscripts with the highest level of agreement (over 90%) are the following:

1739	1891	93.0%	429	522	91.1%
945	1739	92.7%	945	1704	91.0%
322	323	92.1%	945	1891	90.5%
630	2200	91.7%	630	1891	90.4%

Each of the relationships noted here is remarkable in that it is exceptional for any manuscripts outside the Byzantine tradition to have this high level of agreement with others. Of the eight pairs listed above, only two (429/522 and 322/323) are representatives of the Byzantine textual tradition in Acts. Codex 945 agrees with three other manuscripts (1739 1704 and 1891) over 90%, as does manuscript 1891 (1739 945 and 630). Codices 630 (2200 and 1891) and 1739 (1891 and 945) surpass the 90% level with two others. Codices 322 and 323 occur only once each and, in fact, neither one of them agrees with another manuscript over 80%. Manuscripts 429 and 522 also occur only once in the above list. The next level of agreement (exceeding 85%) includes:

1891	2200	88.9%	206	522	85.8%
206	429	87.7%	1739	2200	85.7%
630	1739	87.0%	1704	1739	85.6%
1704	1891	86.9%	429	630	85.1%
630	945	86.1%			

Codices 630 1739 and 1891 are the only manuscripts that exceed an 85% agreement with five others. Codex 522, which had only one agreement surpassing 90%, has only one other over 85% (206). Manuscript 206 (429 and 522) and Codex 429 (206 and 630) have only two agreements that exceed 85%. The only pair that seems to cross the textual traditions is the last one, 429 and 630. Codex 429 belongs primarily to the Byzantine textual tradition in Acts while Codex 630 is a witness for the Egyptian text. It was noted in the first chapter, however, that 630 has been influenced significantly by the Byzantine text in Acts. Only 453 is absent from both of the lists above.

The next two tables demonstrate how the manuscripts relate to each other in the two halves of Acts. In the first half of Acts (Table 19) all the manuscripts agree with the others over 70%. Codices 206 and 453 are the only ones that do not agree with at least one other manuscript 90% and the spread under 453 is again much smaller than for any others. The highest level of agreement in these fourteen chapters is between 1739 and 1891 (94.3%). The manuscripts in the highest level of agreement (over 90%) include:

1739	1891	94.3%		945	1891	91.8%
945	1704	93.1%		322	323	91.1%
945	1739	92.4%		429	522	90.6%
630	2200	91.9%				

Codex 945 has three agreements exceeding 90% (1704 1739 and 1891) while 1739 (1891 and 945) and 1891 (1739 and 945) each has two. The manuscripts in the next level (over 85%) are:

630	1891	89.1%		429	2200	86.5%
429	630	88.8%		1739	2200	86.3%
522	630	87.9%		945	2200	85.8%
1704	1891	87.8%		429	945	85.7%
630	1739	87.5%		429	1739	85.6%
1891	2200	87.3%		522	1891	85.3%
1704	1739	87.3%		630	1704	85.2%
630	945	86.8%		522	2200	85.2%
429	1891	86.7%				

Codices 630 and 1891 agree with seven others over 85%, while 429 945 1739 and 2200 each agree with six others over 85%. The only manuscripts excluded from both lists are 206 and 453, but Codices 322 and 323 again occur only once, agreeing with each other 91.1%.

About one third of the family readings (55 of 155, see pp. 101–111) occur in the first half of Acts. Thus in chapters 1–14, the manuscripts are aligned under their basic textual affinities, without great influence from the family readings.

In the second half of Acts (Table 20), the percentages of agreement are generally higher. Only 453 does not exceed the 89% level of agreement with at least one other manuscript, attaining a high of only 76.2% with 2200. The difference between the top and bottom of the column under this manuscript is even smaller in the second half of Acts than it was for chapters 1–14. A striking difference between Table 19 and Table 20 is the column under 206. This manuscript's highest percentage of agreement in the first fourteen chapters was 81.4% (with 322 and 429). In chapters 15–28, it agrees with Codex 429 93.2% and with 522 91.9%. This will be addressed more fully later (pp. 87ff).

Table 19
Acts 1–14

206		322		323	
322	81.4	323	91.1	322	91.1
429	81.4	206	81.4	1739	81.4
2200	79.5	1704	79.6	1891	80.0
522	79.1	429	78.7	945	79.5
1704	78.8	630	77.9	1704	79.1
630	78.7	1739	77.9	429	78.8
323	77.5	2200	77.6	630	78.6
1891	76.9	522	76.5	206	77.5
945	76.7	1891	76.4	2200	76.7
1739	75.3	945	76.1	522	76.5
453	70.8	453	71.8	453	73.8
429		**453**		**522**	
522	90.6	1891	77.7	429	90.6
630	88.8	1739	76.8	630	87.9
1891	86.7	630	74.9	1891	85.3
2200	86.5	2200	74.9	2200	85.2
945	85.7	945	74.5	1739	84.2
1739	85.6	429	74.3	945	83.9
1704	84.5	323	73.8	1704	82.8
206	81.4	1704	72.7	206	79.1
323	78.8	522	72.6	322	76.5
322	78.7	322	71.8	323	76.5
453	74.3	206	70.8	453	72.6
630		**945**		**1704**	
2200	91.9	1704	93.1	945	93.1
1891	89.1	1739	92.4	1891	87.8
429	88.8	1891	91.8	1739	87.3
522	87.9	630	86.8	630	85.2
1739	87.5	2200	85.8	2200	84.8
945	86.8	429	85.7	429	84.5
1704	85.2	522	83.9	522	82.8
206	78.7	323	79.5	322	79.6
323	78.6	206	76.7	323	79.1
322	77.9	322	76.1	206	78.8
453	74.9	453	74.5	453	72.7
1739		**1891**		**2200**	
1891	94.3	1739	94.3	630	91.9
945	92.4	945	91.8	1891	87.3
630	87.5	630	89.1	429	86.5
1704	87.3	1704	87.8	1739	86.3
2200	86.3	2200	87.3	945	85.8
429	85.6	429	86.7	522	85.2
522	84.2	522	85.3	1704	84.8
323	81.4	323	80.0	206	79.5
322	77.9	453	77.7	322	77.6
453	76.8	206	76.9	323	76.7
206	75.3	322	76.4	453	74.9

Family 1739 in Acts

Table 20
Acts 15–28

206		322		323	
429	93.2	323	93.0	322	93.0
522	91.9	429	77.8	429	77.0
630	82.5	1704	76.8	1704	76.9
2200	82.0	206	76.7	206	75.7
1891	81.4	522	75.8	522	75.1
1704	80.5	2200	75.6	2200	74.9
945	77.2	630	73.8	1891	74.4
1739	76.9	1891	72.8	630	74.3
322	76.7	453	71.7	1739	73.1
323	75.7	945	70.8	945	73.0
453	71.9	1739	70.7	453	72.1
429		**453**		**522**	
206	93.2	2200	76.2	206	91.9
522	91.5	1891	75.7	429	91.5
2200	82.3	630	74.8	630	79.9
630	81.9	1739	74.7	1704	79.0
1891	81.2	945	73.2	2200	79.0
1704	80.8	429	73.0	1891	78.5
322	77.8	1704	72.4	322	75.8
945	77.3	323	72.1	945	75.5
323	77.0	206	71.9	323	75.1
1739	76.7	322	71.7	1739	74.8
453	73.0	522	71.7	453	71.7
630		**945**		**1704**	
2200	91.6	1739	93.0	945	89.2
1891	91.5	1891	89.4	1891	86.1
1739	86.6	1704	89.2	1739	84.2
945	85.6	630	85.6	2200	84.0
1704	83.7	2200	83.6	630	83.7
206	82.5	429	77.3	429	80.8
429	81.9	206	77.2	206	80.5
522	79.9	522	75.5	522	79.0
453	74.8	453	73.2	323	76.9
323	74.3	323	73.0	322	76.8
322	73.8	322	70.8	453	72.4
1739		**1891**		**2200**	
945	93.0	1739	91.9	630	91.6
1891	91.9	630	91.5	1891	90.2
630	86.6	2200	90.2	1739	85.1
2200	85.1	945	89.4	1704	84.0
1704	84.2	1704	86.1	945	83.6
206	76.9	206	81.4	429	82.3
429	76.7	429	81.2	206	82.0
522	74.8	522	78.5	522	79.0
453	74.7	453	75.7	453	76.2
323	73.1	323	74.4	322	75.6
322	70.7	322	72.8	323	74.9

The highest level of agreement for the latter fifteen chapters is between 206 and 429 (93.2%), followed closely by 945 and 1739 (93.0%) and 322 and 323 (93.0%). 1891 is the only one to agree with three others óver 90% and it agrees with a fourth manuscript 89.4%. Notice the large jumps in the columns under 206 and 429. 206 drops from 91.9% to 82.5% between 522 and 630, and 429 goes from 91.5% with 522 to 82.3% with 2200. The manuscripts included in the highest level of agreement (over 90%) are:

206	429	93.2%	630	2200	91.6%
322	323	93.0%	429	522	91.5%
945	1739	93.0%	630	1891	91.5%
206	522	91.9%	1891	2200	90.2%
1739	1891	91.9%			

Manuscript 945 occurs only once in this list (with 1739); Codex 1739 agrees with two others (945 and 1891) over 90%; and 1891 reaches this level of agreement with three others (1739 630 and 2200). Codex 206 does not agree with any of the other manuscripts as much as 85% in the first half of Acts, but in the second half it agrees with two others, 429 and 522, over 90%. Codices 429 and 522 maintain approximately the same level in the latter fifteen chapters as they had in chapters 1–14, as do manuscripts 322 and 323. The manuscripts in the second level (over 85%) include:

945	1891	89.4%	630	945	85.6%
945	1704	89.2%	630	1739	86.6%
1704	1891	86.1%	1739	2200	85.1%

1891 agrees with five others over 85%, while 630 945 and 1739 each agrees with four others over 85%. The only manuscript excluded from the two lists for chapters 15–28 is 453.

One hundred of the 155 Family 1739 readings occur in the second half of Acts. Thus there is significantly more influence from the family readings in chapters 15–28 than in the first half of the book. In the next several tables percentages of agreement for each of the manuscripts for different sections of Acts are presented.

In chapters 1–6 (Table 21), 206 and 453 are the only manuscripts not to exceed the 89.9% level of agreement with any other manuscript. This is even more significant with regard to 453, since it does not reach even the 80% level. The lowest level of agreement is between 453 and 522 (69.7%). 429 and 522 agree with each other 90.2% of the time,

Table 21
Acts 1–6

206		322		323	
322	85.2	323	90.6	322	90.6
429	80.8	206	85.2	1739	81.9
323	80.2	429	81.7	1891	81.0
2200	79.5	2200	80.4	429	80.8
630	78.3	1704	80.3	945	80.5
1704	77.9	630	79.9	206	80.2
522	76.2	1739	79.3	1704	78.3
1891	76.1	1891	78.5	630	77.6
945	75.8	522	77.6	2200	77.2
1739	74.2	945	77.4	522	76.5
453	71.9	453	73.3	453	74.2
429		453		522	
522	90.2	1891	77.2	429	90.2
630	88.1	1739	75.3	630	86.1
2200	86.3	323	74.2	2200	83.0
1739	84.9	2200	73.7	1739	82.7
945	84.0	322	73.3	1891	81.3
1891	82.5	429	73.0	945	80.8
322	81.7	945	72.3	1704	78.1
206	80.8	630	72.1	322	77.6
323	80.8	206	71.9	323	76.5
1704	80.4	1704	70.3	206	76.2
453	73.0	522	69.7	453	69.7
630		945		1704	
2200	89.9	1739	92.7	945	92.3
429	88.1	1704	92.3	1891	86.5
522	86.1	1891	89.5	1739	86.4
1739	85.2	2200	86.7	630	83.1
1891	84.9	630	84.2	2200	83.1
945	84.2	429	84.0	429	80.4
1704	83.1	522	80.8	322	80.3
322	79.9	323	80.5	323	78.3
206	78.3	322	77.4	522	78.1
323	77.6	206	75.8	206	77.9
453	72.1	453	72.3	453	70.3
1739		1891		2200	
1891	93.0	1739	93.0	630	89.9
945	92.7	945	89.5	1739	86.9
2200	86.9	1704	86.5	945	86.7
1704	86.4	630	84.9	429	86.3
630	85.2	2200	84.1	1891	84.1
429	84.9	429	82.5	1704	83.1
522	82.7	522	81.3	522	83.0
323	81.9	323	81.0	322	80.4
322	79.3	322	78.5	206	79.5
453	75.3	453	77.2	323	77.2
206	74.2	206	76.1	453	73.7

Table 22
Acts 7–10

206		322		323	
322	81.5	323	91.5	322	91.5
429	76.7	206	81.5	1739	82.5
323	76.1	1704	79.3	1704	81.1
2200	75.3	1739	79.0	945	81.0
630	74.8	429	78.8	1891	81.0
522	74.6	630	77.6	630	80.0
1704	73.8	945	77.2	429	78.8
1891	71.7	1891	77.2	522	77.0
1739	71.6	522	76.6	206	76.1
945	69.5	2200	75.6	2200	75.4
453	68.2	453	71.8	453	75.1
429		**453**		**522**	
522	90.7	1891	77.5	429	90.7
630	90.7	1739	77.3	630	89.3
1891	88.6	630	76.9	1891	87.0
2200	86.9	2200	76.5	2200	86.4
1739	86.3	522	75.5	1739	85.9
1704	84.5	429	75.3	945	83.2
945	83.6	323	75.1	1704	82.9
322	78.8	945	74.6	323	77.0
323	78.8	1704	73.8	322	76.6
206	76.7	322	71.8	453	75.5
453	75.3	206	68.2	206	74.6
630		**945**		**1704**	
2200	92.1	1739	93.7	945	93.5
429	90.7	1704	93.5	1739	89.7
1891	90.7	1891	91.9	1891	88.7
522	89.3	630	86.5	630	85.6
1739	89.1	429	83.6	429	84.5
945	86.5	522	83.2	2200	83.3
1704	85.6	2200	82.0	522	82.9
323	80.0	323	81.0	323	81.1
322	77.6	322	77.2	322	79.3
453	76.9	453	74.6	206	73.8
206	74.8	206	69.5	453	73.8
1739		**1891**		**2200**	
1891	95.2	1739	95.2	630	92.1
945	93.7	945	91.9	1891	88.5
1704	89.7	630	90.7	429	86.9
630	89.1	1704	88.7	522	86.4
429	86.3	429	88.6	1739	85.4
522	85.9	2200	88.5	1704	83.3
2200	85.4	522	87.0	945	82.0
323	82.5	323	81.0	453	76.5
322	79.0	453	77.5	322	75.6
453	77.3	322	77.2	323	75.4
206	71.6	206	71.7	206	75.3

and 630 and 2200 agree 89.9%. The highest level of agreement in this section is between 1739 945 and 1891 (1739 is more closely related to the other two than they are to each other) and between 945 and 1704. 945 and 1739 are the only manuscripts in this section that agree with two others over 90%. The highest percentages of agreement (over 90%) in chapters 1–6 are:

1739	1891	93.0%	322	323	90.6%
1739	945	92.7%	429	522	90.2%
945	1704	92.3%			

The next level (over 85%) consists of the following:

630	2200	89.9%	1704	1739	86.4%
945	1891	89.5%	429	2200	86.3%
429	630	88.1%	522	630	86.1%
1739	2200	86.9%	206	322	85.2%
945	2200	86.7%	630	1739	85.2%
1704	1891	86.5%			

1739 is the only manuscript in this section that agrees with five others over 85%. The only manuscript excluded completely from these two groups is 453.

This section of Acts (along with 11–14) is the least affected by the Family 1739 readings; there are only seventeen in these six chapters, six primary Family 1739 readings and eleven secondary ones (see pp. 101–111). As can be seen in Appendix I, this section is also the one in which the Byzantine tradition had the most influence on these late minuscules. It is no surprise, then, that the percentages of agreement among the ten manuscripts are somewhat lower than in other sections.

Again, in Table 22, 206 and 453 do not exceed the 90% level of agreement with any other manuscript of the study. The highest level of agreement in chapters 7–10 is between 1739 and 1891 (95.2%) and this is followed closely by 1739 and 945 (93.7%). Once again, it is clear that 1739 is more closely related to 945 and 1891 than those two manuscripts are to each other. The lowest level of agreement in this section is 68.2% (between 206 and 453).

The manuscripts agreeing with others over 90% are:

1739	1891	95.2%	630	2200	92.1%
1739	945	93.7%	945	1891	91.9%
945	1704	93.5%	322	323	91.5%

429	522	90.7%			
429	630	90.7%			
630	1891	90.7%			

The next level (over 85%) contains the following manuscripts:

1704	1739	89.7%	429	2200	86.9%
522	630	89.3%	630	945	86.5%
630	1739	89.1%	522	2200	86.4%
1704	1891	88.7%	429	1739	86.3%
429	1891	88.6%	522	1739	85.9%
1891	2200	88.5%	630	1704	85.6%
522	1891	87.0%			

Three manuscripts, Codices 630 1739 and 1891, agree with seven other manuscripts over 85%. Once again, 453 is not included in these lists. This section has only a few more Family 1739 readings (21) than the first section.

In chapters 11–14 (Table 23), Codex 453 is the only one not to reach an 80% level of agreement with any other manuscript. The highest level of agreement exists between 1739 and 1891 (94.5%), between 945 and 1739 (93.9%), between 630 and 2200 (93.9%), and between 945 and 1704 (93.6%). For the first time, all the manuscripts agree with all the others at least 70.0%. The highest agreements (over 90%) in these chapters are among the following manuscripts:

1739	1891	94.5%	429	522	91.0%
945	1891	93.9%	429	945	90.5%
630	2200	93.9%	945	1739	90.2%
945	1704	93.6%	630	1891	90.8%
322	323	91.3%			

The next level (over 85%) consists of the following manuscripts:

630	945	89.9%	1704	1891	87.8%
1891	2200	89.2%	522	1704	87.7%
429	1704	88.9%	630	1739	87.6%
945	2200	88.8%	522	1891	87.1%
522	945	88.6%	206	945	87.0%
429	1891	88.5%	630	1704	86.9%
206	429	88.4%	429	630	86.8%
206	522	88.3%	1739	2200	86.7%
1704	2200	88.2%	522	2200	86.4%
522	630	87.8%	429	2200	86.2%

206	1704	85.8%	1704	1739	85.4%
429	1739	85.6%			

Codices 429 945 and 1704 agree with eight other manuscripts over 85%. Clearly there is a higher level of agreement among the manuscripts of the group in this section than in the previous two sections. In chapters 1–6, there were five agreements over 90% and eleven over 85%; in chapters 7–10, there were nine agreements over 90% and fourteen over 85%. In this section (11–14), there are nine over 90% and twenty–three over 85%. Obviously something has changed among the manuscripts in this section of Acts. Since there are not significantly more Family 1739 readings in this section (17 readings), the change is due more to declining Byzantine influence on most of the manuscripts, as can be observed in Appendix I.

In chapters 15–19 (Table 24), Codex 453 continues to be the only manuscript that fails to reach an 80% level of agreement with any others. In the previous section, 206 had moved up into the high 80's, but here it makes an even more impressive move upward with 429 (92.1%) and 522 (91.3%). Like the last section, none of the manuscripts fall below a 70% level of agreement with the rest.

The highest level of agreement (over 90%) in these chapters consists of the following manuscripts:

1739	1891	95.3%	206	429	92.1%
945	1704	94.4%	630	1891	91.6%
322	323	93.5%	206	522	91.3%
630	2200	92.5%	429	522	90.5%
945	1739	92.3%	1891	2200	90.4%
945	1891	92.2%			

The next level of agreement (over 85%) contains the following:

429	2200	89.0%	1739	2200	87.3%
429	630	88.6%	630	945	86.7%
630	1739	88.5%	522	630	86.0%
1704	1891	88.2%	206	1739	85.7%
206	1891	88.1%	429	945	85.6%
206	2200	88.1%	206	945	85.3%
1704	1739	87.8%	429	1739	85.1%
429	1891	87.7%	945	2200	85.0%
206	630	87.7%	1704	2200	85.0%

Table 23
Acts 11–14

206		322		323	
429	88.4	323	91.3	322	91.3
522	88.3	1704	79.3	1739	79.3
945	87.0	206	76.7	1891	77.8
1704	85.8	2200	76.4	630	77.7
630	84.4	630	76.3	1704	77.5
1891	84.2	429	75.1	2200	77.5
2200	83.7	1739	75.0	429	76.5
1739	81.2	522	74.9	945	76.3
322	76.7	1891	73.2	206	76.0
323	76.0	945	73.1	522	75.7
453	72.8	453	70.0	453	71.6

429		453		522	
522	91.0	1891	78.5	429	91.0
945	90.5	1739	77.6	945	88.6
1704	88.9	945	77.0	206	88.3
1891	88.5	630	75.2	630	87.8
206	88.4	2200	74.8	1704	87.7
630	86.8	429	74.5	1891	87.1
2200	86.2	1704	73.9	2200	86.4
1739	85.6	206	72.8	1739	83.6
323	76.5	522	72.2	323	75.7
322	75.1	323	71.6	322	74.9
453	74.5	322	70.0	453	72.2

630		945		1704	
2200	93.9	1891	93.9	945	93.6
1891	90.8	1704	93.6	429	88.9
945	89.9	429	90.5	2200	88.2
522	87.8	1739	90.2	1891	87.8
1739	87.6	630	89.9	522	87.7
1704	86.9	2200	88.8	630	86.9
429	86.8	522	88.6	206	85.8
206	84.4	206	87.0	1739	85.4
323	77.7	453	77.0	322	79.3
322	76.3	323	76.3	323	77.5
453	75.2	322	73.1	453	73.9

1739		1891		2200	
1891	94.5	1739	94.5	630	93.9
945	90.2	945	93.9	1891	89.2
630	87.6	630	90.8	945	88.8
2200	86.7	2200	89.2	1704	88.2
429	85.6	429	88.5	1739	86.7
1704	85.4	1704	87.8	522	86.4
522	83.6	522	87.1	429	86.2
206	81.2	206	84.2	206	83.7
323	79.3	453	78.5	323	77.5
453	77.6	323	77.8	322	76.4
322	75.0	322	73.2	453	74.8

Family 1739 in Acts

Table 24
Acts 15–19

206		322		323	
429	92.1	323	93.5	322	93.5
522	91.3	2200	78.4	2200	78.4
1891	88.1	1704	76.1	1739	77.9
2200	88.1	630	75.8	1891	77.9
630	87.7	429	75.6	429	77.2
1739	85.7	1739	75.3	630	77.2
945	85.3	1891	75.3	1704	76.7
1704	84.3	945	74.0	945	76.6
323	75.0	522	73.9	206	75.0
322	73.6	206	73.6	522	74.8
453	73.0	453	70.6	453	72.4
429		**453**		**522**	
206	92.1	1891	78.7	206	91.3
522	90.5	1739	78.6	429	90.5
2200	89.0	630	77.7	630	86.0
630	88.6	2200	76.6	1891	84.6
1891	87.7	945	75.7	2200	84.4
945	85.6	1704	74.2	945	83.4
1739	85.1	429	73.5	1704	83.1
1704	84.9	206	73.0	1739	82.7
323	77.2	323	72.4	323	74.8
322	75.6	522	71.1	322	73.9
453	73.5	322	70.6	453	71.1
630		**945**		**1704**	
2200	92.5	1704	94.4	945	94.4
1891	91.6	1739	92.3	1891	88.2
429	88.6	1891	92.2	1739	87.8
1739	88.5	630	86.7	2200	85.0
206	87.7	429	85.6	429	84.9
945	86.7	206	85.3	630	84.4
522	86.0	2200	85.0	206	84.3
1704	84.4	522	83.4	522	83.1
453	77.7	323	76.6	323	76.7
323	77.2	453	75.7	322	76.1
322	75.8	322	74.0	453	74.2
1739		**1891**		**2200**	
1891	95.3	1739	95.3	630	92.5
945	92.3	945	92.2	1891	90.4
630	88.5	630	91.6	429	89.0
1704	87.8	2200	90.4	206	88.1
2200	87.3	1704	88.2	1739	87.3
206	85.7	206	88.1	945	85.0
429	85.1	429	87.7	1704	85.0
522	82.7	522	84.6	522	84.4
453	78.6	453	78.7	322	78.4
323	77.9	323	77.9	323	78.4
322	75.3	322	75.3	453	76.6

There are slightly fewer manuscripts represented in these two lists than in the last section, with only one more in the first group. 206 429 630 945 1739 1891 and 2200 all agree with seven others over 85%. This section of Acts contains twenty–eight Family 1739 readings.

In Table 25, Codex 453 remains the only manuscript that does not exceed an 80% level of agreement with any other manuscript, while Codices 322 323 453 1704 and 1739 all fall below 70% with at least one other witness. The level of agreement between 945 and 1739 is striking–94.3%. The highest level of agreement in this section (over 90%) contains the following manuscripts:

945	1739	94.3%	322	323	92.1%
206	429	93.5%	630	2200	91.3%
1739	1891	92.8%	945	1704	91.3%
630	1891	92.4%	429	522	91.0%
206	522	92.1%	1891	2200	90.1%

The next level of agreement contains the following witnesses:

945	1891	89.8%	1704	1739	86.7%
630	1739	89.7%	1739	2200	86.3%
630	945	88.2%	1704	1891	85.2%
206	630	86.9%	206	1891	85.0%

Interestingly, there are far fewer manuscripts in this second level, while the higher level maintained a consistent number. Codex 1891 agrees with six others over 85% and Codices 630 and 1739 agree with five others over 85%.

This section contains more Family 1739 readings than any other section in Acts. It is no surprise, then, to see the very high agreement between 1739 and 945, and also between 206 and 429.

In Table 26, there are several places where the level of agreement falls below 70%, most notably, 206–1739 (58.3%), 429–1739 (60.2%), and 522–1739 (58.3%). Another interesting change is the decrease of agreement of 1891 with both 945 and 1739. It has been consistently over 90%, but decreases here to 85.9% (1739) and 85.1% (945). The highest level of agreement (exceeding 90%) consists of the following:

206	429	94.1%	945	1739	92.1%
429	522	93.3%	630	2200	90.6%
322	323	93.3%	1891	2200	90.0%
206	522	92.4%	630	1891	90.0%

Table 25
Acts 20–24

206		322		323	
429	93.5	323	92.1	322	92.1
522	92.1	1704	74.3	1704	75.5
630	86.9	206	74.0	2200	73.3
1891	85.0	429	73.3	206	72.4
2200	84.7	2200	73.1	429	72.4
1739	81.6	630	72.3	630	72.4
945	81.2	522	72.0	1739	72.3
1704	80.5	453	70.2	945	71.6
322	74.0	1891	70.0	1891	71.4
323	72.4	1739	69.4	522	70.8
453	71.4	945	69.3	453	69.3
429		453		522	
206	93.5	2200	76.3	206	92.1
522	91.0	630	73.7	429	91.0
630	84.6	1739	73.2	630	83.8
2200	83.5	1891	72.7	2200	81.8
1891	82.7	429	71.9	1891	81.5
1739	80.2	206	71.4	945	78.5
945	79.7	522	71.2	1739	78.4
1704	78.0	945	71.2	1704	78.1
322	73.3	322	70.2	322	72.0
323	72.4	323	69.3	453	71.2
453	71.9	1704	69.1	323	70.8
630		945		1704	
1891	92.4	1739	94.3	945	91.3
2200	91.3	1704	91.3	1739	86.7
1739	89.7	1891	89.8	1891	85.2
945	88.2	630	88.2	630	84.8
206	86.9	2200	84.0	2200	82.3
1704	84.8	206	81.2	206	80.5
429	84.6	429	79.7	522	78.1
522	83.8	522	78.5	429	78.0
453	73.7	323	71.6	323	75.5
323	72.4	453	71.2	322	74.3
322	72.3	322	69.3	453	69.1
1739		1891		2200	
945	94.3	1739	92.8	630	91.3
1891	92.8	630	92.4	1891	90.1
630	89.7	2200	90.1	1739	86.3
1704	86.7	945	89.8	206	84.7
2200	86.3	1704	85.2	945	84.0
206	81.6	206	85.0	429	83.5
429	80.2	429	82.7	1704	82.3
522	78.4	522	81.5	522	81.8
453	73.2	453	72.7	453	76.3
323	72.3	323	71.4	323	73.3
322	69.4	322	70.0	322	73.1

Table 26
Acts 25–28

206		322		323	
429	94.1	323	93.3	322	93.3
522	92.4	429	86.7	429	82.7
322	84.7	206	84.7	206	80.9
323	80.9	522	83.3	522	80.9
1704	75.1	1704	80.5	1704	79.0
453	71.0	453	75.2	453	75.1
2200	70.3	2200	74.3	1891	73.4
630	69.2	630	73.0	630	72.6
1891	67.1	1891	73.0	2200	71.6
945	60.6	945	68.2	945	69.6
1739	58.3	1739	65.9	1739	67.2

429		453		522	
206	94.1	2200	75.4	429	93.3
522	93.3	322	75.2	206	92.4
322	86.7	323	75.1	322	83.3
323	82.7	1891	75.1	323	80.9
1704	78.1	429	73.8	1704	74.4
453	73.8	1704	73.5	453	73.0
2200	71.3	522	73.0	2200	68.8
1891	69.8	630	72.1	630	66.7
630	68.7	945	72.0	1891	66.6
945	62.3	1739	71.2	945	61.1
1739	60.2	206	71.0	1739	59.5

630		945		1704	
2200	90.6	1739	92.1	1891	84.2
1891	90.0	1891	85.1	2200	84.2
1704	81.6	2200	81.2	630	81.6
945	80.6	630	80.6	322	80.5
1739	79.9	1704	79.6	945	79.6
322	73.0	453	72.0	323	79.0
323	72.6	323	69.6	429	78.1
453	72.1	322	68.2	1739	76.0
206	69.2	429	62.3	206	75.1
429	68.7	522	61.1	522	74.4
522	66.7	206	60.6	453	73.5

1739		1891		2200	
945	92.1	630	90.0	630	90.6
1891	85.9	2200	90.0	1891	90.0
2200	80.6	1739	85.9	1704	84.2
630	79.9	945	85.1	945	81.2
1704	76.0	1704	84.2	1739	80.6
453	71.2	453	75.1	453	75.4
323	67.2	323	73.4	322	74.3
322	65.9	322	73.0	323	71.6
429	60.2	429	69.8	429	71.3
522	59.5	206	67.1	206	70.3
206	58.3	522	66.6	522	68.8

The second level (exceeding 85%) contains the following:

    322   429   86.7%
    945 1891   85.1%
    1739 1891   85.9%

One striking feature of Table 26 is the sharp decrease from the most closely related manuscripts to the others. For instance, under 206 there is the decrease between 522 and 323 from 92.4% to 84.7%. The same phenomenon was observed earlier in Table 20.

Within this last section, several manuscripts have a significant shift in affinities in chapter 28 (See Appendix II). One of the more striking shifts occurs in the relationship between Codices 1739 and 1891. These two agree 95.8% in chapter 25, 94.4% in chapter 26, and 90.8% in chapter 27. That agreement drops remarkably to 62.2% in chapter 28. In that chapter, 1891 agrees with the Majority Text 91.8%, while Codex 1739 maintains its primary affinity with the Egyptian textual tradition. A similar phenomenon occurs between codices 1704 and 1739, though this time it seems to begin in chapter 27. The agreements between those two manuscripts for the last four chapters are: chapter 25–88.7%, 26–84.6%, 27–71.4%, and 28–61.2%. Similarly, 630 and 1739 agree 83.1% in chapter 27, but only 57.3% in chapter 28, and 2200 and 1739 agree 88.2% in chapter 27, and only 59.4% in chapter 28. Corresponding to those changes, each of the four manuscripts that change significantly in the last chapter of Acts has a much higher level of agreement with the Majority Text in that chapter. Codex 1891 probably influenced 630 1704 and 2200, but why 1891 has a strong agreement with the Byzantine textual tradition only in Acts 28 remains unknown.

The tables in this section have suggested three groupings of manuscripts within the twelve that need to be examined further. The first group includes 630 945 1704 1739 1891 and 2200 and these appear to be the primary members of Family 1739. The second group includes 206 429 and 522. These have very significant relationships with each other, especially in chapters 15–28, but they appear to be closer to the Byzantine textual tradition in Acts than to the Egyptian text. The third group consists of 322 and 323. These are not all that significantly related to the other ten manuscripts, but they have a strong level of agreement between the two of them. That leaves only Codex

453, which does not appear to be all that significantly related to the others.

The Manuscripts' Relationships Throughout Acts

In the last nine tables (18–26), the different sections of Acts were the controlling factor in the presentation of the data. For the next twelve, the figures for each manuscript are presented in one chart. In this way the changes in a manuscript's affinities can be seen more clearly. The first three tables (Tables 27–29) give the figures for three very mixed manuscripts (322 323 and 453).

Codex 322's relationship to Codex 323 is striking (Table 27), particularly in view of its unimpressive level of agreement with others of the study. Its level of agreement with 323 extends from 90.6% (chapters 1–6) to 93.5% (chapters 15–19). Other than with 323, its highest level of agreement is with Codex 429 (86.7% in chapters 25–28); its lowest level of agreement is with 1739 (65.9% in chapters 25–28). Table 6 demonstrated that 322 has strong affinity for the Byzantine textual tradition in Acts, agreeing with the control group for that tradition even more than with other manuscripts of this study (excluding, of course, Codex 323). As indicated in the earliers tables, Codex 322 does not have strong affinity for the other manuscripts.

Table 28 shows that Codex 323's highest level of agreement is with 322, never falling below 90.6% in any section. Its lowest level of agreement is with 1739 (67.2%) in chapters 25–28. Excluding 322, for the first half of Acts, it maintains an average of 73.8% to 81.4% with the others and for the second half from 72.1% to 77.0%, and it never agrees with any other manuscript (excluding 322) over 83% for any part of Acts. The relationship of this manuscript to Family 1739 is in question because of its low level of agreement with 1739 945 and 1891 or with any of the other manuscripts more closely related to those. Like 322, Codex 323 is a fairly mixed manuscript with strong affinities for the Byzantine textual tradition in Acts and it contains some Family 1739 readings (see p. 110).

Codex 453 (Table 29) has nowhere near the same level of agreeement with other manuscripts of this study as do the others. Its highest level of agreement is 78.7% (with 1891 in 15–19); its lowest level is 68.2% (206 in 7–10). As with 322 and 323, this manuscript's

Table 27
322

1–6		7–10		11–14	
323	90.6	323	91.5	323	91.3
206	85.2	206	81.5	1704	79.3
429	81.7	1704	79.3	206	76.7
2200	80.4	1739	79.0	2200	76.4
1704	80.3	429	78.8	630	76.3
630	79.9	630	77.6	429	75.1
1739	79.3	945	77.2	1739	75.0
1891	78.5	1891	77.2	522	74.9
522	77.6	522	76.6	1891	73.2
945	77.4	2200	75.6	945	73.1
453	73.3	453	71.8	453	70.0
15–19		**20–24**		**25–28**	
323	93.5	323	92.1	323	93.3
2200	78.4	1704	74.3	429	86.7
1704	76.1	206	74.0	206	84.7
630	75.8	429	73.3	522	83.3
429	75.6	2200	73.1	1704	80.5
1739	75.3	630	72.3	453	75.2
1891	75.3	522	72.0	2200	74.3
945	74.0	453	70.2	630	73.0
522	73.9	1891	70.0	1891	73.0
206	73.6	1739	69.4	945	68.2
453	70.6	945	69.3	1739	65.9
1–14		**15–28**		**1–28**	
323	91.1	323	93.0	323	92.1
206	81.4	429	77.8	206	78.9
1704	79.6	1704	76.8	429	78.2
429	78.7	206	76.7	1704	78.1
630	77.9	522	75.8	2200	76.5
1739	77.9	2200	75.6	522	76.1
2200	77.6	630	73.8	630	75.7
522	76.5	1891	72.8	1891	74.4
1891	76.4	453	71.7	1739	74.0
945	76.1	945	70.8	945	73.3
453	71.8	1739	70.7	453	71.8

Table 28
323

1–6		7–10		11–14	
322	90.6	322	91.5	322	91.3
1739	81.9	1739	82.5	1739	79.3
1891	81.0	1704	81.1	1891	77.8
429	80.8	945	81.0	630	77.7
945	80.5	1891	81.0	1704	77.5
206	80.2	630	80.0	2200	77.5
1704	78.3	429	78.8	429	76.5
630	77.6	522	77.0	945	76.3
2200	77.2	206	76.1	206	76.0
522	76.5	2200	75.4	522	75.7
453	74.2	453	75.1	453	71.6
15–19		**20–24**		**25–28**	
322	93.5	322	92.1	322	93.3
2200	78.4	1704	75.5	429	82.7
1739	77.9	2200	73.3	206	80.9
1891	77.9	206	72.4	522	80.9
429	77.2	429	72.4	1704	79.0
630	77.2	630	72.4	453	75.1
1704	76.7	1739	72.3	1891	73.4
945	76.6	945	71.6	630	72.6
206	75.0	1891	71.4	2200	71.6
522	74.8	522	70.8	945	69.6
453	72.4	453	69.3	1739	67.2
1–14		**15–28**		**1–28**	
322	91.1	322	93.0	322	92.1
1739	81.4	429	77.0	1704	77.9
1891	80.0	1704	76.9	429	77.8
945	79.5	206	75.7	1739	76.9
1704	79.1	522	75.1	1891	76.9
429	78.8	2200	74.9	206	76.5
630	78.6	1891	74.4	630	76.2
206	77.5	630	74.3	945	76.0
2200	76.7	1739	73.1	522	75.8
522	76.5	945	73.0	2200	75.7
453	73.8	453	72.1	453	72.9

Table 29
453

1–6		7–10		11–14	
1891	77.2	1891	77.5	1891	78.5
1739	75.3	1739	77.3	1739	77.6
323	74.2	630	76.9	945	77.0
2200	73.7	2200	76.5	630	75.2
322	73.3	522	75.5	2200	74.8
429	73.0	429	75.3	429	74.5
945	72.3	323	75.1	1704	73.9
630	72.1	945	74.6	206	72.8
206	71.9	1704	73.8	522	72.2
1704	70.3	322	71.8	323	71.6
522	69.7	206	68.2	322	70.0
15–19		20–24		25–28	
1891	78.7	2200	76.3	2200	75.4
1739	78.6	630	73.7	322	75.2
630	77.7	1739	73.2	323	75.1
2200	76.6	1891	72.7	1891	75.1
945	75.7	429	71.9	429	73.8
1704	74.2	206	71.4	1704	73.5
429	73.5	522	71.2	522	73.0
206	73.0	945	71.2	630	72.1
323	72.4	322	70.2	945	72.0
522	71.1	323	69.3	1739	71.2
322	70.6	1704	69.1	206	71.0
1–14		15–28		1–28	
1891	77.7	2200	76.2	1891	76.6
1739	76.8	1891	75.7	1739	75.7
630	74.9	630	74.8	2200	75.6
2200	74.9	1739	74.7	630	74.8
945	74.5	945	73.2	945	73.8
429	74.3	429	73.0	429	73.6
323	73.8	1704	72.4	323	72.9
1704	72.7	323	72.1	1704	72.5
522	72.6	206	71.9	522	72.1
322	71.8	322	71.7	322	71.8
206	70.8	522	71.7	206	71.4

relationship to Family 1739 is questionable. However, 453 also agrees on the average at least 70% with the other manuscripts of the study in the two halves of Acts. Codex 453, too, is a very mixed manuscript, having just a slightly greater affinity for the Egyptian textual tradition.

The next three tables (Tables 30–32) provide the figures for three manuscripts that belong primarily to the Byzantine textual tradition in Acts. These three tables will be followed by six others including manuscripts belonging primarily to the Egyptian textual tradition of Acts.

When the percentages for 206 are presented in this format, it is clear that there is a shift in this manuscript's affinities at 11–14. Its highest level of agreement in chapters 1–6 is 85.2% (322) and in chapters 7–10, it is 81.5% (322). However in 11–14 it goes up to 88.4% (429) and is then at 92.1% (429) for 15–19. In chapters 15–28, 206 has at least a 92.0% agreement with 429. Its highest level of agreement is with 429 and 522, and that agreement is significantly higher in chapters 15–28 than in 1–14. Appendix I indicates that its percentage of agreement with the Majority text is the most obvious change between the two halves of the book, occurring primarily between chapters 11 and 12. In Acts 1–11, 206 agrees with the Majority Text between 85% and 96%. In chapter 12, 206's agreement with the Majority Text is only 68.7 and that percentage fluctuates between 65% and 75% from chapter 12 through 23. This change in the relationship between 206 and the Byzantine tradition involves some important changes elsewhere. For instance, its agreement with 429 changes dramatically between chapter 11 (77.6%) and 12 (92.5%); the same is true for 206 and 522–chapter 11 (77.6%), chapter 12 (94.0%). There are other shifts that fit this same pattern. For instance, through chapter 11 the highest level of agreement of 206 with 1891 is 82.1% (chapter 6) and its average agreement with 1891 is in the low to mid 70's. From chapter 12 through 27, it averages in the mid to upper 80's. This pattern reflects well that only one of this manuscript's Family 1739 readings falls outside chapters 12–23. 206's general relationship with 945 1739 and 1891 is low. The highest level reached is 88.1% (1891 in 15–19), and the low is with 1739 at 58.3% (in chapters 25–28). This manuscript's change in its relationship with 1739 is a shift that will be observed with several of the manuscripts. In chapters 1–6, the two manuscripts agree only 74.2%; that remains

Table 30
206

1–6		7–10		11–14	
322	85.2	322	81.5	429	88.4
429	80.8	429	76.7	522	88.3
323	80.2	323	76.1	945	87.0
2200	79.5	2200	75.3	1704	85.8
630	78.3	630	74.8	630	84.4
1704	77.9	522	74.6	1891	84.2
522	76.2	1704	73.8	2200	83.7
1891	76.1	1891	71.7	1739	81.2
945	75.8	1739	71.6	322	76.7
1739	74.2	945	69.5	323	76.0
453	71.9	453	68.2	453	72.8
15–19		20–24		25–28	
429	92.1	429	93.5	429	94.1
522	91.3	522	92.1	522	92.4
1891	88.1	630	86.9	322	84.7
2200	88.1	1891	85.0	323	80.9
630	87.7	2200	84.7	1704	75.1
1739	85.7	1739	81.6	453	71.0
945	85.3	945	81.2	2200	70.3
1704	84.3	1704	80.5	630	69.2
323	75.0	322	74.0	1891	67.1
322	73.6	323	72.4	945	60.6
453	73.0	453	71.4	1739	58.3
1–14		15–28		1–28	
322	81.4	429	93.2	429	87.7
429	81.4	522	91.9	522	85.8
2200	79.5	630	82.5	630	80.8
522	79.1	2200	82.0	2200	80.8
1704	78.8	1891	81.4	1704	79.7
630	78.7	1704	80.5	1891	79.3
323	77.5	945	77.2	322	78.9
1891	76.9	1739	76.9	945	77.0
945	76.7	322	76.7	323	76.5
1739	75.3	323	75.7	1739	76.2
453	70.8	453	71.9	453	71.4

Table 31
429

1–6		7–10		11–14	
522	90.2	522	90.7	522	91.0
630	88.1	630	90.7	945	90.5
2200	86.3	1891	88.6	1704	88.9
1739	84.9	2200	86.9	1891	88.5
945	84.0	1739	86.3	206	88.4
1891	82.5	1704	84.5	630	86.8
322	81.7	945	83.6	2200	86.2
206	80.8	322	78.8	1739	85.6
323	80.8	323	78.8	323	76.5
1704	80.4	206	76.7	322	75.1
453	73.0	453	75.3	453	74.5
15–19		**20–24**		**25–28**	
206	92.1	206	93.5	206	94.1
522	90.5	522	91.0	522	93.3
2200	89.0	630	84.6	322	86.7
630	88.6	2200	83.5	323	82.7
1891	87.7	1891	82.7	1704	78.1
945	85.6	1739	80.2	453	73.8
1739	85.1	945	79.7	2200	71.3
1704	84.9	1704	78.0	1891	69.8
323	77.2	322	73.3	630	68.7
322	75.6	323	72.4	945	62.3
453	73.5	453	71.9	1739	60.2
1–14		**15–28**		**1–28**	
522	90.6	206	93.2	522	91.1
630	88.8	522	91.5	206	87.7
1891	86.7	2200	82.3	630	85.1
2200	86.5	630	81.9	2200	84.2
945	85.7	1891	81.2	1891	83.7
1739	85.6	1704	80.8	1704	82.5
1704	84.5	322	77.8	945	81.2
206	81.4	945	77.3	1739	80.8
323	78.8	323	77.0	322	78.2
322	78.7	1739	76.7	323	77.8
453	74.3	453	73.0	453	73.6

Table 32

522

1–6		7–10		11–14	
429	90.2	429	90.7	429	91.0
630	86.1	630	89.3	945	88.6
2200	83.0	1891	87.0	206	88.3
1739	82.7	2200	86.4	630	87.8
1891	81.3	1739	85.9	1704	87.7
945	80.8	945	83.2	1891	87.1
1704	78.1	1704	82.9	2200	86.4
322	77.6	323	77.0	1739	83.6
323	76.5	322	76.6	323	75.7
206	76.2	453	75.5	322	74.9
453	69.7	206	74.6	453	72.2
15–19		**20–24**		**25–28**	
206	91.3	206	92.1	429	93.3
429	90.5	429	91.0	206	92.4
630	86.0	630	83.8	322	83.3
1891	84.6	2200	81.8	323	80.9
2200	84.4	1891	81.5	1704	74.4
945	83.4	945	78.5	453	73.0
1704	83.1	1739	78.4	2200	68.8
1739	82.7	1704	78.1	630	66.7
323	74.8	322	72.0	1891	66.6
322	73.9	453	71.2	945	61.1
453	71.1	323	70.8	1739	59.5
1–14		**15–28**		**1–28**	
429	90.6	206	91.9	429	91.1
630	87.9	429	91.5	206	85.8
1891	85.3	630	79.9	630	83.6
2200	85.2	1704	79.0	2200	81.9
1739	84.2	2200	79.0	1891	81.6
945	83.9	1891	78.5	1704	80.8
1704	82.8	945	75.5	945	79.5
206	79.1	323	75.1	1739	79.1
322	76.5	322	75.8	322	76.1
323	76.5	1739	74.8	323	75.8
453	72.6	453	71.7	453	72.1

consistent (at 71.6%) in 7–10, increases significantly to 81.2% in 11–14 to a high of 85.7% in 15–19; there is a slight decrease to 81.6% in 20–24, and a dramatic drop to 58.3% in chapters 25–28. Appendix II shows that this change occurs specifically in chapter 24. The most significant change in manuscript 206 between chapters 23 and 24 is in its relationship to the Byzantine tradition. In chapter 23, 206 and the MT agree only 66.3%, but in chapter 24 that jumps to 86.2% and stays on that level for the rest of the book.

Codex 429 is clearly the manuscript most closely related to 206. Its percentage of agreement with 206 averages 93.2% for chapters 15–28 with a high of 94.1% in chapters 25–28. Codex 522 is close behind, averaging 91.5% for chapters 15–28. It would thus appear that for chapters 15–28, 206 429 and 522 have a close enough agreement to be considered a "family" in Acts. More will be said about this later. The same dramatic change in agreement with 1739, seen earlier with 206, occurs with 429 also. Notice how in chapters 20–24 manuscript 429 agrees with 1739 80.2%, but falls to 60.2% in chapters 25–28. Again, that change takes place at chapter 24 (Appendix II), and is characterized by a marked increase in agreement between 429 and MT. The decrease in agreement with 1739 is paralleled by a decrease in 429's agreement with 2200 630 945 and 1891–all basically Egyptian witnesses–and an increase with 206 522 322 and 323–all basically Byzantine witnesses. Manuscripts 429 and 522 never fall below a 90.2% level of agreement. Codex 206, because of its own fluctuation between the first and second halves of Acts has an unimpressive relationship with 429 in the first half, but a very significant one in the second half, always over 92.0%. Again, the three manuscripts, 429 522 and 206 (for chapters 11–28), maintain a relationship over 90%. Though not nearly as consistent as those, another significant relationship is noted here; Codices 630 (7–10) and 945 (11–14) each attain a 90% level of agreement with 429 once.

In Table 32, the relationship between 206 429 and 522 is observed from 522's direction. As is now expected, the relationship between 206 and 522 is much higher in chapters 15–28 than in 1–14, while the relationship between 429 and 522 remains consistently over 90%. Also, the decline in relationship with 1739 945 1891 and 2200 that was noted with 206 and 429 is seen here.

These last three manuscripts (206 429 and 522) are drawn together from two directions: 1) they share several Family 1739 readings in common and 2) more significantly, they are strongly influenced by the Byzantine textual tradition in Acts. The high level of agreement is not all that unusual in manuscripts of that tradition, as seen earlier in the relationships between H L P 049 and 105.

Codex 630 has a relationship with 2200 of 89.9% or above throughout Acts, and with 1891 that exceeds 90% for chapters 11–28. Interestingly, given the close relationship between 1739 and 1891, 630 and 1739 reach a high level of 89.7% in chapters 20–24, but that drops to a low of 79.9% in chapters 25–28. Since its relationship with 1891 remains consistent, clearly 630 has an unusually high agreement with the Majority Text in chapter 28 (85.4%), like 1891 does (90.8%–see Appendix II). Its relationship with 429 exceeds 90% for chapters 7–10 and is generally very high for chapters 1–10, but it decreases fairly steadily from that point. 630's level of agreement with 945 is 89.9% in chapters 11–14, up from the mid–80's in chapters 1–10; it remains consistently high for chapters 15–24 and then drops significantly in the last section. This is because of 630's higher level of agreement with the Byzantine tradition in chapter 28. For chapters 25–27, the percentage of agreement with 945 is 87.0%; for chapter 28 it is 60.4%. This is the same general pattern 630 follows in relation to 1739; these two agree 86.9% in chapters 25–27 and 57.3% in chapter 28. Because both 1891 and 2200 are also much closer to the Byzantine tradition in chapter 28, 630's relationship to those manuscripts remains fairly constant. Codex 522 agrees with 630 in the mid to upper 80's in chapters 1–19, then decreases slightly in chapters 20–24, and dramatically in chapters 25–28. This is the typical pattern of 630 with also 206 429 and 522. This pattern recurs because very few Family 1739 readings occur in these three manuscripts in the latter portions of Acts.

945 (Table 34) has an agreement of 92% or more with 1739 in all of Acts and its highest level of agreement is 94.4% (with 1704 in 15–19); its lowest level of agreement is with 206 (60.6% in 25–28). Codex 945 agrees with 1891 89.5% or more for the first 24 chapters, but falls to 85.1% in 25–28. This is because of 1891's radical change of affinities in chapter 28; in chapters 25–27, 945 agrees with 1891 over 92%, but only 63.3% in chapter 28 where 1891 has a 90.8%

Table 33
630

1–6		7–10		11–14	
2200	89.9	2200	92.1	2200	93.9
429	88.1	429	90.7	1891	90.8
522	86.1	1891	90.7	945	89.9
1739	85.2	522	89.3	522	87.8
1891	84.9	1739	89.1	1739	87.6
945	84.2	945	86.5	1704	86.9
1704	83.1	1704	85.6	429	86.8
322	79.9	323	80.0	206	84.4
206	78.3	322	77.6	323	77.7
323	77.6	453	76.9	322	76.3
453	72.1	206	74.8	453	75.2
15–19		**20–24**		**25–28**	
2200	92.5	1891	92.4	2200	90.6
1891	91.6	2200	91.3	1891	90.0
429	88.6	1739	89.7	1704	81.6
1739	88.5	945	88.2	945	80.6
206	87.7	206	86.9	1739	79.9
945	86.7	1704	84.8	322	73.0
522	86.0	429	84.6	323	72.6
1704	84.4	522	83.8	453	72.1
453	77.7	453	73.7	206	69.2
323	77.2	323	72.4	429	68.7
322	75.8	322	72.3	522	66.7
1–14		**15–28**		**1–28**	
2200	91.9	2200	91.6	2200	91.7
1891	89.1	1891	91.5	1891	90.4
429	88.8	1739	86.6	1739	87.0
522	87.9	945	85.6	945	86.1
1739	87.5	1704	83.7	429	85.1
945	86.8	206	82.5	1704	84.4
1704	85.2	429	81.9	522	83.6
206	78.7	522	79.9	206	80.8
323	78.6	453	74.8	323	76.2
322	77.9	323	74.3	322	75.7
453	74.9	322	73.8	453	74.8

Table 34
945

1–6		7–10		11–14	
1739	92.7	1739	93.7	1891	93.9
1704	92.3	1704	93.5	1704	93.6
1891	89.5	1891	91.9	429	90.5
2200	86.7	630	86.5	1739	90.2
630	84.2	429	83.6	630	89.9
429	84.0	522	83.2	2200	88.8
522	80.8	2200	82.0	522	88.6
323	80.5	323	81.0	206	87.0
322	77.4	322	77.2	453	77.0
206	75.8	453	74.6	323	76.3
453	72.3	206	69.5	322	73.1
15–19		20–24		25–28	
1704	94.4	1739	94.3	1739	92.1
1739	92.3	1704	91.3	1891	85.1
1891	92.2	1891	89.8	2200	81.2
630	86.7	630	88.2	630	80.6
429	85.6	2200	84.0	1704	79.6
206	85.3	206	81.2	453	72.0
2200	85.0	429	79.7	323	69.6
522	83.4	522	78.5	322	68.2
323	76.6	323	71.6	429	62.3
453	75.7	453	71.2	522	61.1
322	74.0	322	69.3	206	60.6
1–14		15–28		1–28	
1704	93.1	1739	93.0	1739	92.7
1739	92.4	1891	89.4	1704	91.0
1891	91.8	1704	89.2	1891	90.5
630	86.8	630	85.6	630	86.1
2200	85.8	2200	83.6	2200	84.6
429	85.7	429	77.3	429	81.2
522	83.9	206	77.2	522	79.5
323	79.5	522	75.5	323	76.0
206	76.7	453	73.2	206	77.0
322	76.1	323	73.0	453	73.8
453	74.5	322	70.8	322	73.3

agreement with the Majority Text. 945 follows that same pattern with 630 (87.0% for chapters 25–27 and 60.4% for chapter 28) and 2200 (86.4% for chapters 25–27 and 64.6% for chapter 28). 945 follows the same pattern as was observed with 630 in regard to 206 429 and 522.

1704's highest level of agreement (Table 35) is with 945, agreeing with it 91.0% of the time in the entire book. That agreement is somewhat higher in the first half (93.1%) than in the second (89.2%) and that is accounted for primarily by the decrease in agreement in chapters 25–28 (79.6%). The tables in Appendix II indicate that the drop actually occurred between chapters 23 (94.1%) and 24 (86.5%), but changed dramatically at chapter 27 (75.6%) and 28 (67.3%). That is paralleled by 1704's increase in agreement with the Majority Text in the last two chapters (27–86.6%; 28–94.9%). 1704's agreement with 1739, in chapters 1–24, extends from a low of 85.4% (chapters 11–14) to a high of 89.7% (7–10). Its level of agreement with 1891 is in the same range, but remains consistent in chapters 25–28 because of 1891's own increase of agreement with the Byzantine tradition in that section.

Codex 1739 (Table 36) maintains a percentage of agreement with 945 of at least 90.2% for the entire book and its highest level of agreement with 945 occurs in chapters 20–24 (94.3%). Its level of agreement with 1891 is 92.8% or above for Acts 1–24 and falls below 90% only in chapters 25–28 and that is, again, because of 1891's dramatic move toward the Byzantine tradition in chapter 28.   In chapters 25–27, 1739 and 1891 agree 93.4%; in chapter 28, 62.2%. 1739 follows this same pattern with 630 (86.9% in 25–27; 57.3% in 28) and 2200 (87.3% in 25–27 and 59.4% in 28) because both of them share 1891's affinity for the Byzantine tradition in the last chapter. 1739's lowest level of agreement is with 206 in chapters 25–28 (58.3%). It follows the same general pattern as 630 and 945 in relation to manuscripts 206 429 and 522, again because very few Family 1739 readings occur in the latter chapters of Acts in those manuscripts.

Codex 1891 (Table 37) has a consistently high level of agreement with 1739 and 945, exceeding 90% except for chapters 25–28. In 11–28 it agrees with 2200 from 89.2% to 90.4%. Its lowest level of agreement is with 522 in chapters 25–28 (66.6%). In general, 1891 has a higher level of agreement with 206 429 and 522 than 1739 because it has been influenced more by the Byzantine textual tradition than 1739, particularly, as has been mentioned frequently, in chapter 28. While its

Table 35
1704

1–6		7–10		11–14	
945	92.3	945	93.5	945	93.6
1891	86.5	1739	89.7	429	88.9
1739	86.4	1891	88.7	2200	88.2
630	83.1	630	85.6	1891	87.8
2200	83.1	429	84.5	522	87.7
429	80.4	2200	83.3	630	86.9
322	80.3	522	82.9	206	85.8
323	78.3	323	81.1	1739	85.4
522	78.1	322	79.3	322	79.3
206	77.9	206	73.8	323	77.5
453	70.3	453	73.8	453	73.9
15–19		**20–24**		**25–28**	
945	94.4	945	91.3	1891	84.2
1891	88.2	1739	86.7	2200	84.2
1739	87.8	1891	85.2	630	81.6
2200	85.0	630	84.8	322	80.5
429	84.9	2200	82.3	945	79.6
630	84.4	206	80.5	323	79.0
206	84.3	522	78.1	429	78.1
522	83.1	429	78.0	1739	76.0
323	76.7	323	75.5	206	75.1
322	76.1	322	74.3	522	74.4
453	74.2	453	69.1	453	73.5
1–14		**15–28**		**1–28**	
945	93.1	945	89.2	945	91.0
1891	87.8	1891	86.1	1891	86.9
1739	87.3	1739	84.2	1739	85.6
630	85.2	2200	84.0	630	84.4
2200	84.8	630	83.7	2200	84.4
429	84.5	429	80.8	429	82.5
522	82.8	206	80.5	522	80.8
322	79.6	522	79.0	206	79.7
323	79.1	323	76.9	322	78.1
206	78.8	322	76.8	323	77.9
453	72.7	453	72.4	453	72.5

Table 36
1739

1–6		7–10		11–14	
1891	93.0	1891	95.2	1891	94.5
945	92.7	945	93.7	945	90.2
2200	86.9	1704	89.7	630	87.6
1704	86.4	630	89.1	2200	86.7
630	85.2	429	86.3	429	85.6
429	84.9	522	85.9	1704	85.4
522	82.7	2200	85.4	522	83.6
323	81.9	323	82.5	206	81.2
322	79.3	322	79.0	323	79.3
453	75.3	453	77.3	453	77.6
206	74.2	206	71.6	322	75.0
15–19		**20–24**		**25–28**	
1891	95.3	945	94.3	945	92.1
945	92.3	1891	92.8	1891	85.9
630	88.5	630	89.7	2200	80.6
1704	87.8	1704	86.7	630	79.9
2200	87.3	2200	86.3	1704	76.0
206	85.7	206	81.6	453	71.2
429	85.1	429	80.2	323	67.2
522	82.7	522	78.4	322	65.9
453	78.6	453	73.2	429	60.2
323	77.9	323	72.3	522	59.5
322	75.3	322	69.4	206	58.3
1–14		**15–28**		**1–28**	
1891	94.3	945	93.0	1891	93.0
945	92.4	1891	91.9	945	92.7
630	87.5	630	86.6	630	87.0
1704	87.3	2200	85.1	2200	85.7
2200	86.3	1704	84.2	1704	85.6
429	85.6	206	76.9	429	80.8
522	84.2	429	76.7	522	79.1
323	81.4	522	74.8	323	76.9
322	77.9	453	74.7	206	76.2
453	76.8	323	73.1	453	75.7
206	75.3	322	70.7	322	74.0

Table 37
1891

1–6		7–10		11–14	
1739	93.0	1739	95.2	1739	94.5
945	89.5	945	91.9	945	93.9
1704	86.5	630	90.7	630	90.8
630	84.9	1704	88.7	2200	89.2
2200	84.1	429	88.6	429	88.5
429	82.5	2200	88.5	1704	87.8
522	81.3	522	87.0	522	87.1
323	81.0	323	81.0	206	84.2
322	78.5	453	77.5	453	78.5
453	77.2	322	77.2	323	77.8
206	76.1	206	71.7	322	73.2
15–19		**20–24**		**25–28**	
1739	95.3	1739	92.8	630	90.0
945	92.2	630	92.4	2200	90.0
630	91.6	2200	90.1	1739	85.9
2200	90.4	945	89.8	945	85.1
1704	88.2	1704	85.2	1704	84.2
206	88.1	206	85.0	453	75.1
429	87.7	429	82.7	323	73.4
522	84.6	522	81.5	322	73.0
453	78.7	453	72.7	429	69.8
323	77.9	323	71.4	206	67.1
322	75.3	322	70.0	522	66.6
1–14		**15–28**		**1–28**	
1739	94.3	1739	91.9	1739	93.0
945	91.8	630	91.5	945	90.5
630	89.1	2200	90.2	630	90.4
1704	87.8	945	89.4	2200	88.9
2200	87.3	1704	86.1	1704	86.9
429	86.7	206	81.4	429	83.7
522	85.3	429	81.2	522	81.6
323	80.0	522	78.5	206	79.3
453	77.7	453	75.7	323	76.9
206	76.9	323	74.4	453	76.6
322	76.4	322	72.8	322	74.4

Table 38
2200

1–6		7–10		11–14	
630	89.9	630	92.1	630	93.9
1739	86.9	1891	88.5	1891	89.2
945	86.7	429	86.9	945	88.8
429	86.3	522	86.4	1704	88.2
1891	84.1	1739	85.4	1739	86.7
1704	83.1	1704	83.3	522	86.4
522	83.0	945	82.0	429	86.2
322	80.4	453	76.5	206	83.7
206	79.5	322	75.6	323	77.5
323	77.2	323	75.4	322	76.4
453	73.7	206	75.3	453	74.8
15–19		**20–24**		**25–28**	
630	92.5	630	91.3	630	90.6
1891	90.4	1891	90.1	1891	90.0
429	89.0	1739	86.3	1704	84.2
206	88.1	206	84.7	945	81.2
1739	87.3	945	84.0	1739	80.6
945	85.0	429	83.5	453	75.4
1704	85.0	1704	82.3	322	74.3
522	84.4	522	81.8	323	71.6
322	78.4	453	76.3	429	71.3
323	78.4	323	73.3	206	70.3
453	76.6	322	73.1	522	68.8
1–14		**15–28**		**1–28**	
630	91.9	630	91.6	630	91.7
1891	87.3	1891	90.2	1891	88.9
429	86.5	1739	85.1	1739	85.7
1739	86.3	1704	84.0	945	84.6
945	85.8	945	83.6	1704	84.4
522	85.2	429	82.3	429	84.2
1704	84.8	206	82.0	522	81.9
206	79.5	522	79.0	206	80.8
322	77.6	453	76.2	322	76.5
323	76.7	322	75.6	323	75.7
453	74.9	323	74.9	453	75.6

agreements with 945 and 1739 drop sharply in chapter 28, its level of agreement with 630 (90.2% for 25–27; 89.6% for 28) and 2200 (89.8% for 25–27; 89.6% for 28) decreases only slightly, indicating once again that these three share a sharp increase in agreement with the Byzantine textual tradition in Acts 28.

Codex 2200 (Table 38) agrees with 630 89.9% and higher for the whole of Acts, and it exeeds the 90% level of agreement with 1891 in chapters 15–28.   Its consistent level of agreement with 1891 in chapters 25–28 indicates a significant shift toward the Byzantine tradition in chapter 28.

Summary

Codex 453, though somewhat significantly related to the others, does not have a strong enough relationship to be considered a leading member of the family. As will be shown in the next section, it contains a few of the family readings, but it is already clear that it is a "cousin" at best.

Codices 322 and 323 are also no more than "cousins" to the other manuscripts in Family 1739. They, too, share some of the family readings, but are only marginally related to the family as a whole. They are, however, very significantly related to each other.

Among the other nine manuscripts, very significant relationships surface. There are four relationships in particular that bear watching in the next section: a) 1739 1891 and 945; b) 945 and 1704; c) 630 and 2200 (with 1891 for chapters 15–28); and d) 429 and 522 (with 206 for the latter half of Acts). The percentages of agreement for the manuscripts in each of these three groups exceeds 90% for an extended time.

Family 1739 Readings

For any group of manuscripts to be considered a "family," the manuscripts must share readings that are unique to that group. On the following pages are the Family 1739 readings in Acts. They are divided into two groups: those that are found only in members of

Family 1739 and those found in Family 1739 and a few other witnesses. The reading before the square bracket is that of NA²⁶ and UBS³.

Primary Family 1739 Readings

(1st occurrence <u>underlined</u>; last occurrence <u>underlined</u>)

1. 1.22   τῆς ἡμέρας ἧς] ἧς ἡμέρας <u>323</u> <u>945</u> <u>1704</u>
2. 2.30   καθίσαι] ἀνάστησεν τὸν Χριστὸν καθίσαι (323) (<u>429</u>) 1704 <u>1739</u> <u>1891</u>
3. 3.18   - αὐτοῦ <u>322</u> 429 <u>522</u> <u>630</u> 945 1704 1739 1891 <u>2200</u>
4. 4.14   βλέποντες σὺν αὐτοῖς] σὺν αὐτοῖς βλέποντες 429 522 630 945 1704 1739 1891 2200
5. 5.32   ἐσμὲν μάρτυρες] ἐν αὐτῷ μάρτυρες (429) 522 630 945 1704 1739 (1891)
6. 5.40   ἐπί] ἐν 322 323 945 1704 1739 1891
7. 7.2   ἀκούσατε] ἀκούσατε μοῦ 322 323 429 <u>453</u> 945 1704 1739 1891 2200
8. 7.4   ὑμεῖς νῦν] νῦν ὑμεῖς 429 630 945 1704 1739 1891 2200
9. 7.5   αὐτόν] αὐτῆς 945 1704 1739 1891 2200
10. 7.36   τέρατα καὶ σημεῖα] σημεῖα καὶ τέρατα 429 522 630 945 1704 1739 1891
11. 7.42   ἔτη τεσσεράκοντα ἐν τῇ ἐρήμῳ] ἐν τῇ ἐρήμῳ τεσσεράκοντα 322 323 429 453 522 630 945 1704 1739 1891
12. 9.13   - ἀπό 945 1704 1739 1891 2200
13. 9.21   ἀγάγῃ] ἀπαγάγῃ 429 522 630 945 1704 1739 1891 (2200)
14. 9.33   ἐκεῖ ἄνθρωπον] ἄνθρωπον ἐκεῖ 945 1704 1739 1891
15. 10.16   τὸ σκεῦος] ἅπαντα 429 630 1739 1891 2200
16. 10.25   πόδας] πόδας αὐτοῦ 323 429 522 630 945 1704 1739 1891 2200
17. 10.30   μέχρι] ἄχρι 429 522 630 945 1704 1739 1891 2200
18. 10.30   ἐνώπιον] ἐναντίον 429 522 630 945 1704 1739 1891 2200
19. 10.32   μετακάλεσαι] μεταπέμψαι 429 522 630 945 1704 1739 1891 2200

20. 10.32   Σίμωνος] Σίμωνός τινος 429 522 630 945 1704 1739 1891 2200

21. 11.13   ἄγγελον] ἄγγελον τοῦ θεοῦ 322 323 429 453 522 630 945 1704 1739 1891 2200

22. 12.11   κύριος] θεός <u>206</u> 322 323 429 453 522 630 945 1704 1739 1891 2200

23. 13.7   θεοῦ] κυρίου 429 522 630 945 1704 1739 1891 2200

24. 13.31   μάρτυρες αὐτοῦ] αὐτοῦ μάρτυρες 206 429 522 630 945 1704 1739 1891 2200

25. 14.22   ἐμμένειν] ἐπιμένειν 206 429 522 630 945 1704 1891 2200

26. 15.20   καὶ τῆς πορνείας καὶ τοῦ πνικτοῦ καὶ τοῦ αἵματος] καὶ τοῦ αἵματος καὶ τοῦ πνικτοῦ καὶ τῆς πορνείας 206 429 522 630 945 1704 1739 1891 2200

27. 15.26   αὐτῶν] ἑαυτῶν (206) 322 323 429 (522) 945 1704 1739 1891 2200

28. 17.5   πόλιν] πόλιν κατ' αὐτῶν 206 322 323 429 522 630 945 1704 1739 1891 2200

29. 17.15   ἤγαγον] ἦλθον 206 429 522 630 945 1704 1739 1891 2200

30. 17.18   ἀνάστασιν] ἀνάστασιν αὐτοῦ 206 322 323 429 522 630 945 1704 1739 1891 2200

31. 17.26   προστεταγμένους] τεταγμένους 206 322 323 429 522 630 945 1704 1739 1891 2200

32. 18.17   τῷ Γαλλίωνι ἔμελεν] ἔμελλε τῷ Γαλλίωνι 206 429 630 945 1704 1739 1891 2200

33. 18.26   τὴν ὁδὸν τοῦ θεοῦ] τὸν λόγον τοῦ κυρίου 322 323 945 1704 1739 1891
(τὸν λόγον τοῦ θεοῦ 429 522 630 2200)

34. 19.16   κατακυριεύσας] κατεκυρίευσεν 206 429 630 945 1704 1739 1891 2200

35. 19.16   ἴσχυσεν] καὶ ἴσχυσεν 206 429 522 630 945 1704 1739 1891

36. 19.17   γνωστὸν πᾶσιν] πᾶσιν γνωστόν 206 429 522 630 945 1704 1739 1891 2200

37. 19.34   ἐπιγνόντες] ἐπιγνόντων 206 429 453 630 945 1704 1739 1891 (TR)

38. 20.1 μεταπεμψάμενος] μεταστειλάμενος 206 429 630 945
1704 1739 1891 2200
39. 20.3 εἰς] ἐπί 206 429 630 945 1704 1891 2200
40. 20.7 μέχρι] ἄχρι 206 429 522 630 945 1704 1739 1891 2200
41. 20.10 συμπεριλαβών] συμπεριλαβὼν αὐτόν 206 322 323 429
453 945 1704 1739 1891 2200
42. 20.25 τὴν βασιλείαν] τὸ εὐαγγέλιον 206 322 323 429 522 630
945 1704 1739 1891
43. 20.26 εἰμί] ἐγώ εἰμι 206 429 522 945 1704 1891
44. 20.32 δυναμένῳ] δυναμένῳ ὑμᾶς 206 322 323 429 522 630 945
1704 1739 1891
45. 21.6 ἀπησπασάμεθα] ἠσπασάμεθα 206 429 522 630 945 1739
1891
46. 21.18 ἐπιούσῃ] ἐπαύριον 206 429 522 630 945 1739 1891 2200
47. 21.18 πρεσβύτεροι] πρεσβύτεροι πρὸς αὐτόν (429) 945 1739
(2200)
48. 21.24 τὴν κεφαλήν] τὰς κεφαλάς 206 322 323 429 522 630 945
1739ᶜ 1891 2200
49. 21.26 προσηνέχθη] προσενέχθη 206 322 323 429 630 945ᵛⁱᵈ
1704 1739 1891 2200
50. 22.5 εἰς¹] ἐν 945 1739 1891
51. 22.13 κἀγώ] καὶ ἐγώ 206 429 522 630 945 1704 1739 1891 2200
52. 22.23 αὐτῶν] αὐτῶν ἐπὶ πλεῖον 206 429 522 630 945 1704
1739 1891 2200
53. 23.1 ἡμέρας] ὥρας 206 429 522 630 945 1704 1739 1891 2200
54. 23.6 Σαδδουκαίων τὸ δὲ ἕτερον Φαρισαίων] Φαρισαίων τὸ δὲ
ἕτερον Σαδδουκαίων 522 630 945 1704 1739 1891
2200
55. 23.18 ἠρώτησεν] ἤρωτα 945 1704 1739 1891
56. 24.19 - ἐπὶ σοῦ 630 1739 1891 2200
57. 24.20 ἀδίκημα] ἀδίκημα ἐν ἐμοί (429) 630 945 1704 1739
1891 2200
58. 24.21 σήμερον ἐφ᾽ ὑμῶν] ὑφ᾽ ὑμῶν σήμερον (429) 630 945 1704
1739 1891 2200
59. 24.22 διαγνώσομαι] ἀκριβέστερον διαγνώσομαι 322 323 630
945 1704 1739 1891 2200
60. 25.5 ἐν τῷ ἀνδρὶ ἄτοπον] ἄτοπον ἐν τῷ ἀνδρί 322 323 630
945 1704 1739 1891 2200

61. 26.10   τῶν ἁγίων ἐγώ] ἐγὼ τῶν ἁγίων   630 945 1704 1739
     1891 2200
62. 26.13   μέσης] μεσούσης   630 945 1704 1739 1891 2200
63. 26.18   φῶς] τὸ φῶς   630 945 1704 1739 1891 2200
64. 26.18   σκότους] τοῦ σκότους   <u>453</u> 945 1704 1739 1891ᶜ 2200
65. 26.20   ἀπήγγελλον] κατήγγελλον   322 323 630 945 1704 1739
     1891 2200
66. 26.26   τούτων²] ἐγὼ τούτων   945 1704 1739 1891
67. 27.7   μὴ προσεῶντος] οὐκ ἐῶντος   <u>322</u> <u>323</u> 945 1704 1739
     1891 2200
68. 27.8   τε] δέ   630 945 <u>1704</u> <u>1739</u> 1891 2200
69. 27.33   δὲ οὖ] οὖν   <u>630</u> 945 1739 <u>1891</u> <u>2200</u>
70. 28.5   ἔπαθεν] ἔπασχεν   <u>945</u> <u>1739</u>

What is noteworthy about this first set of readings is how "unspectacular" they are. Few of them are the kind of reading that strikes one as intentional (only nos. 26, 33, and 42 might fit that description), and yet there is certainly more than coincidence at work here. Interestingly, although reading 37 is clearly a family reading, it became the reading in the *Textus Receptus*.

Below are presented the number of these seventy readings that each of the twelve manuscripts of the present study contains:

     945 – 67
     1739– 66 (not extant for no. 1)
     1891– 66
     1704– 61 (lacuna at 4)
     2200– 53 (lacuna at 4)
     630 – 52
     429 – 48
     522 – 35
     206 – 28 (between nos. 22 and 53, it includes 28 of 32)
     323 – 22
     322 – 20
     453 – 5

These numbers demonstrate clearly that 945 1739 1891 and 1704 are the leading members of the family, with 2200 630 and 429 on the second level. 522 contains exactly half the readings, while 206 and 323 fall well below half. Between numbers 22 and 53 (that is Acts 12:11–

23:1) 206 contains 28 of the 32 family readings. It contains none before 12:11 and none after 23:1. Codex 453 contains only 5 of the primary family readings.

Below are presented different combinations of manuscripts and how often each combination occurs in support of the seventy family readings.

945 1739 1891 – 58
945 1704 1739 1891 – 55
630 945 1739 1891 – 47
945 1739 1891 2200 – 45
630 945 1704 1739 1891 – 44
630 945 1739 1891 2200 – 41
630 945 1704 1739 1891 2200 – 39
429 630 945 1739 1891 – 39
429 522 630 945 1739 1891 – 28
206 429 522 630 945 1739 1891 – 18
206 322 323 429 522 630 945 1739 1891 – 6
206 323 429 453 522 630 945 1739 1891 – 1
206 322 323 429 453 522 630 945 1704 1739 1891 2200 – 1

This shows, as expected, that 945 1739 and 1891 appear most often in support of these readings. More than half the readings are supported by a group that includes those three, plus 630 1704 2200 and 429.

Finally, one family reading is supported only by 945 1739 and 1891 (no. 14); three are supported by only 945 1704 1739 and 1891 (50, 55, 66); four family readings are supported only by 630 945 1704 1739 1891 and 2200 (nos. 61, 62, 63, 68); and one is supported only by 630 945 1739 1891 and 2200 (69).

Below are presented what are called "secondary Family 1739 readings." These are readings for which the main support is manuscripts from this family, but which also have some support from a few other manuscripts.

106   *Family 1739 in Acts*

Secondary Family 1739 Readings

(1st occurrence <u>underlined</u>; last occurrence <u>underlined</u>)

1. 2.38   ἐπὶ τῷ] ἐν τῷ B C D <u>429</u> 522 <u>630</u> <u>945</u> <u>1704</u> <u>1739</u> <u>1891</u>
            <u>2200</u>
2. 2.38   Ἰησοῦ Χριστοῦ] τοῦ κυρίου'Ἰησοῦ Χριστοῦ D E 429 522
            614 630 945 1704 1739 1891 2200 2412
3. 2.47   ἐπὶ τὸ αὐτο] τῇ ἐκκλησίᾳ ἐπὶ τὸ αὐτό 69 429 522 630
            945 1704 1739 1891
4. 3.2   θύραν] πύλην E 181 <u>323</u> 429 522 630 945 1704 1739 1891
            2200
5. 3.22   πρὸς τοὺς πατέρας εἶπεν] εἶπεν πρὸς τοὺς πατέρας Ψ
            429 522 630 945 1611 1704 1739 1891 2200
6. 3.26   ὑμῶν] αὐτοῦ 88 <u>322</u> 323 429 522 913 945 1704 1739
            1891 2200
7. 4.18   καλέσαντες] προσκαλεσάμενοι 630 913 945 1704 1739
            1891 2200
8. 4.21   μηδέν] μή D Ψ 945 1704 1739 1891
9. 4.24   ὁμοθυμαδὸν ἦραν φωνήν] ἦραν φωνὴν ὁμοθυμαδόν 69
            945 1704 1739 1891 2200
10. 5.25   ὅτι] λέγων ὅτι 429 <u>453</u> 522 630 945 1704 1739 1874
            1891 2412 (TR)
11. 5.28   ἐπί] ἐν 322 323 1241 1704 1739 1891 2495
12. 7.51   καρδίαις] ταῖς καρδίαις ὑμῶν ℵ (322) (323) 630 945
            1175 1704 1739 1891 2200
13. 9.19   τροφήν] τροφῆς 104 323 945 1175 1292 1704 1739 1891
14. 9.33   εἰς] ἐν H <u>206</u> 429 522 630 945 1241 1704 1739 1891
            (TR)
15. 9.33   - τινά 383 429 522 945 1704 1739 1891 2200
16. 10.11 καθιέμενον] δεδέμενον καὶ καθιέμενον 81 323 429 453
            522 630 (945) 1704 1739 1891 TR
17. 10.12 ἑρπετά] τὰ ἑρπετά 181 326 429 522 630 945 1704 1739
            1874 1891 TR
18. 10.17 - οἱ E 383 945 1704 1739
19. 11.8   κοινόν] κοινόν τι 322 323 429 522 630 913 1739 1891
            2200

20. 11.21 αὐτῶν] αὐτῶν τοῦ ἰᾶσθαι αὐτούς (104) 322 323 429 522
            630 913 945 1704 1739 1891 2200
21. 12.19 δέ] τέ A 206 429 522 630 945 1704 1739 1891 2200
22. 12.21 - ὁ B 88 429 522 630 945 1175 1704 1739 1891 2200
23. 12.25 εἰς᾽ Ἰερουσαλήμ] ἐξ᾽ Ἰερουσαλὴμ εἰς᾽ Ἀντιόχειαν 206 429
            522 630 913 945 1704 1739 1891 2200
24. 13.15 οἱ ἀρχισυνάγωγοι πρὸς αὐτούς] πρὸς αὐτοὺς οἱ
            ἀρχισυνάγωγοι Ψ 104 206 429 522 630 945 1704
            1739 1891 2200
25. 13.19 κατεκληρονόμησεν] κατεκληροδότησεν 206 322 323 429
            522 630 945 1505 1704 1739 1891 2495 (TR)
26. 13.25 ποδῶν] ποδῶν αὐτοῦ 206 429 522 630 945 1611 1704
            1891 2200
27. 13.26 - ταύτης C 453 945 1704 1891 2200
28. 13.47 - σε² p45 206 429 945 1704 1739 1891
29. 14.4   - τῆς πόλεως 206 429 522 630 945 1505 1704 1739 1891
            2200 2495
30. 14.12 τέ] δέ D 181 206 429 630 945 1739 1891 2200
31. 15.17 - ἄν E 206 429 522 630 945 1739 1891 2200
32. 15.20 τοῦ αἵματος] τοῦ αἵματος καὶ ὅσα μὴ θέλετε ἑαυτοῖς
            γίνεσθαι ἑτέροις μὴ ποιεῖν   (D) (322) (323)
            (206) (429) (522) (630) 945 1704 (1739) (1891)
            (2200)
33. 15.29 εἰδωλοθύτων] εἰδωλοθύτου 181 206 429 522 630 945 1505
            1704 1739 1891 2200 2495
34. 15.29 πορνείας] πορνείας καὶ ὅσα μὴ θέλετε ἑαυτοῖς γίνεσθαι
            ἑτέροις μὴ ποιεῖν
            D 206 322 323 429 522 614 630 945 1739 1704
            1891 2200 2412
35. 16.15 παρεκάλεσεν] παρεκαλεῖ 206 429 630 945 1175 1704
            1739 1891 2200
36. 17.27 καὶ γέ] καίτοιγε ℵ 206 322 323 429 522 630 945 1704
            1739 1891 (TR)
37. 18.18 ἀποταξάμενος] ἀποταξάμενος αὐτοῖς 104 206 322 323
            429 522 630 945 1704 1739 1891 2200
38. 18.25 τὴν ὁδόν] τὸν λόγον D 206 322 323 429 453 522 630
            945 1704 1739 1891 2200
39. 19.3   τέ] δέ D Ψ 206 429 522 630 945 1704 1739 1891 2200

40. 19.4   Παῦλος] ὁ Παῦλος   D 181 206 429 453 522 630 945 1505 1704 1739 1891 2200 2495

41. 19.4   Ἰησοῦν]Ἰησοῦν Χριστόν   Ψ (429) 945 1175 1704 1739 1891

42. 19.12   ἤ] καί   88 206 429 522 630 945 1704 1739 1891 2200

43. 19.16   - ἐπ' αὐτούς   E 429 945 1704 1739 1891

44. 19.26   Ἐφέσου] τῆς Ἐφέσου   69 206 429 522 630 945 1175 1704 1739 1891

45. 19.27   - τέ   206 322 323 429 453 522 630 945 1175 1704 1739 1891

46. 19.39   ἐπιζητεῖτε] ζητεῖτε   𝔓74 E 206 429 453 630 945 1704 1739 1891 2200

47. 20.1   ἀσπασάμενος] ἀσπασάμενός τε   206 322 323 383 429 630 945 1505 1704 1739 1891 2200 2412 2495

48. 20.1   - πορεύεσθαι   D E (323) 945 1505 1704 1739 2495

49. 20.16   εἰς] ἐν   D* 206 429 522 630 945 1704 1739 1891 2200

50. 20.22   συναντήσαντα] συμβησόμενα   C 206 429 522 630 945 1175 1704 1739 1891

51. 20.26   πάντων] πάντων ὑμῶν   Evid 104 206 326 429 522 630 945 1704 1739 1891

52. 21.5   - ἐξελθόντες   A 945 1739

53. 21.8   ὄντος] τοῦ ὄντος   206 429 522 630 945 1739 1891 2412 2495 (TR)

54. 21.13   - εἰς Ἰερουσαλήμ   206 322 323 383 429 522 630 945 1739 1891 2200

55. 21.15   ἐπισκευασάμενοι] παρασκευασάμενοι   C 206 429 522 630 945 1175 1739 1891 2200

56. 21.24   ὧν] περὶ ὧν   C 181 206 429 453 522 630 945 1704 1739 1891 2200

57. 21.25   κρίναντες φυλάσσεσθαι αὐτούς] κρίναντες μηδὲν τοιοῦτον τηρεῖν ἀλλὰ φυλάσσεσθαι   181 (206) 322 323 (429) (522) 630 (945) 1739

58. 21.40   σιγῆς γενομένης] γενομένης σιγῆς   B 206 429 522 630 945 1739 1891 2200

59. 22.8   τέ] δέ   D 206 322 323 429 522 945 1704 1739 1891 2200

60. 22.13   ἀνέβλεψα] ἐνέβλεψα   104 630 1611 1739 1891

61. 22.17   μοὶ ὑποστρέψαντι] μὲ ὑποστρέψαντα   104 945 1175 1704 1739 (1891)

62. 22.17 - μοῦ E 206 322 323ᵛⁱᵈ 429 522 630 945 1704 1739 1891 2200

63. 22.22 καθῆκεν] καθήκει Ψ 88 206 429 522 630 945 1704 1739 1891 2200

64. 22.25 ἑστῶτα] ἐφεστῶτα 104 206 322 323 429 630 945 1704 1739 1891 2200

65. 23.2 ἐπέταξεν] ἐκέλευσεν C 88 206 429 453 522 630 945 1704 1739 1891 2200

66. 23.15 - τοῦ² א* E 206 429 522 630 945 1704 1739 1891

67. 24.25 μετακαλέσομαι] μεταπέμψομαι 104 614 630 945 1505 1611 1704 1739 1891 2200 2412 2495

68. 25.3 κατ᾽] παρ᾽ C 453 630 945 1704 1739 1891 2200

69. 25.7 ἅ] τοῦ Παύλου א* Ψ 429 630 945 1739 1891

70. 25.9 δέ] οὖν A 181 630 945 1704 1739 1891 2200

71. 25.11 αὐτοῖς] τούτοις C L 453 630 945 1704 1739 1891 2200

72. 25.16 τινά] τινί C 322 323 630 945 1704 1739 1891

73. 25.26 κυρίῳ] κυρίῳ μου 104 322 323 453 945 1704 1739 1891 2200

74. 26.1 περὶ σεαυτοῦ λέγειν] λέγειν περὶ σεαυτοῦ H 630 945 1704 1739 1891 2200

75. 26.2 ὑπό] παρά 𝔓⁷⁴ 630 945 1704 1739 1891 2200

76. 26.14 εἰς] ἐπί 81 181 630 945 1704 1739 1891 2200

77. 26.26 οὐ πείθομαι οὐθέν, οὐ] οὐδὲν πείθομαι, οὐδέ 69 453 945 1739 1891 2200

78. 27.5 - τήν 429 614 1241 1739 1891 2200 2412

79. 27.22 οὐδεμία] οὐδεμίας 69 322 323 453 945 1739

80. 27.23 ταύτῃ τῇ νυκτί] τῇ νυκτὶ ταύτῃ 325 630 945 1739 1891 (TR)

81. 27.29 ἐκπέσωμεν] ἐκπέσωσιν 81 325 326 630 945 1793 1891 2200 (TR)

82. 28.8 ἐπιθείς] ἐπιθείς τε Ψ 69 945 1175 1739

83. 28.14 εἰς τὴν ῾Ρώμην ἤλθαμεν] ἤλθαμεν εἰς τὴν ῾Ρώμην 𝔓⁷⁴ 81 945 1739

84. 28.23 πρὸς αὐτὸν εἰς τὴν ξενίαν] εἰς τὴν ξενίαν πρὸς αὐτόν 104 913 945 1739

85. 28.31 - πάσης Ψ 945 1505 1611 1739

In general, these eighty–five readings are as "unspectacular" as the earlier 70. However, seven of these readings later became *Textus Receptus* readings (nos. 10, 14, 25, 36, 53, 80, 81).

Manuscript 206 exhibits the same pattern as in the earlier readings. That is, its first family reading in this section (no. 14) occurs at Acts 9:33 (its second one occurs at 12:19) and its last one (no. 66) occurs at 23:15. Clearly this manuscript is much more closely related to the overall family between chapters 12 and 23 than anywhere else (see Appendix II).

Below is shown how many of the 155 total readings (that is, both primary and secondary family readings) each of the manuscripts contains, followed by a percentage of how often each manuscript supports one of the readings where that manuscript is extant. In the column under "secondary" is listed the number of times each manuscript supported one of the 85 "secondary family readings." The column under "primary" shows how many of the "primary family readings" each manuscript contains. Those two numbers are then added together and divided by the number of places that particular manuscript is extant to get the percentage of time each manuscript supports the family readings.

	Secondary	**+ Primary**
1739	83/85	(+65 = 148/154 = 96.1%)
945	81/85	(+67 = 148/155 = 95.5%)
1891	76/85	(+66 = 142/155 = 91.6%)
1704	65/80	(+61 = 126/146 = 86.3%)
630	61/85	(+52 = 113/155 = 72.9%)
2200	52/81	(+53 = 105/147 = 71.4%)
429	56/85	(+48 = 106/155 = 67.1%)
522	46/85	(+35 = 81/155 = 52.3%)
206	36/85	(+28 = 64/155 = 41.3%)
323	23/85	(+22 = 45/155 = 29.0%)
322	21/85	(+20 = 41/155 = 26.5%)
453	4/85	(+5 = 19/155 = 12.3%)

These numbers confirm even more strongly that 945 1704 1739 and 1891 are, by far, the leading members of the family; these are followed on an obviously secondary level by 630 2200 and 429. An intermediate level is occupied by 522 and 206; 322 323 and 453, while at least sharing some of the family readings do not share enough to be considered significant members.

Of the 155 readings that may be considered family 1739 readings, 29 occur in the first nine chapters of Acts and the other 126 occur in the last 19 chapters. This accounts for a rather common trait among these manuscripts, that is, that they tend to be more closely related to their respective larger textual traditions (either Byzantine or Egyptian) in the first third of Acts and more closely related to the family manuscripts after that. Clearly, their agreement with the family readings draws them away from their general affinities and brings them closer to the family.

CONCLUSION

The manuscripts considered in the present study have little to say about the original Greek text of Acts, but they have much to contribute to the awareness of the history of that text between the tenth and sixteenth centuries, primarily regarding the mixture of different types of readings in manuscripts of various textual traditions. Nine manuscripts, six belonging to the Egyptian textual tradition and three to the Byzantine textual tradition, share enough readings of Family 1739 to exhibit a significant relationship among them.

Codices 945 1704 1739 and 1891 comprise the primary level of Family 1739; manuscripts 630 and 2200 make up the secondary level. As was mentioned in the introduction, I was already aware of the relationship existing among 945 1739 and 1891, but this study has confirmed that familial relationship, added 1704 to the family, and recognized 630 and 2200 as a secondary level of that family. These manuscripts, as shown in Chapter I, belong to the Egyptian textual tradition of Acts.

Codices 206 429 and 522 are significantly related to that family, but comprise their own special relationship, particularly 429 and 522. Chapter I demonstrated that these three manuscripts belong primarily to the Byzantine textual tradition in Acts. These manuscripts are "cousins" to Family 1739; their close relationship is created by their allegiance to the tightly controlled Byzantine tradition and their sharing a certain number of Family 1739 readings. That later minuscules from two different textual traditions share such a significant number of Family readings indicates a great deal of mixture occurring within different text-types.

Finally, as scholars continue to move into the "age of the minuscules," information of such witnesses will be increasingly important in ascertaining how still other manuscripts relate to these and

113

to other similar groupings. With the information presented here, it will be fairly easy, after a manuscript has been collated, to determine whether or not it belongs to Family 1739. Other groupings of manuscripts need the same kind of information presented so that the history of the New Testament text can finally be written.

APPENDIX I

In the following pages, the number of each kind of reading from among the genetically significant variations each of the twelve manuscripts supports is shown. Under each manuscript the last column entitled O/S represents those times in which the manuscript is not extant (O=omission) or supports a unique or singular reading (S=singular). Below each table the number of each kind of reading that manuscript supports is provided. For example, at the bottom of the chart under 206 is the phrase "Some Byzantine." This phrase is used to represent those readings in the 147 variation units in which there was any significant Byzantine presence. In the notation 115/138, the 138 represents the number of places in the 147 places where this particular manuscript is extant, minus its singular readings (147 minus the number at the bottom of the last column). The 115 represents the number of times that 206 supports a reading that is supported by several Byzantine manuscripts. "Clearly Byzantine" signifies those readings within the 147 that can be clearly identified as specifically Byzantine readings. That is, they are supported solely, or almost solely, by members of the Byzantine textual tradition. There are 52 clearly identifiable Byzantine readings; 206 is extant at 49 of those places and supports that reading 35 times, or 71.4% of the time. The same process holds also for both the Egyptian and "Western" phrases. There are 57 readings within the 147 that can be identified as specifically Egyptian; there are 70 that can be classified as "Western." The percentages at the bottom of each page were presented in Tables 11-16.

Table 39
206

E	EB	EBW	EW	B	BW	W	O/S
72 74 79	1 2 4	5 16	108 112	3 9 11	10 35 36	56 60 61	14 23 52
83 88 93	6 7 8	103 130	127	15 17 20	43 47 91	76 82 84	54 75 99
96 100	12 13 18			21 22 27	95 98	102 133	107 113
114 116	19 24 25			31 32 33			124
128 131	26 28 29			34 37 38			
	30 39 40			42 69 80			
	41 44 45			87 111			
	46 48 49			119 121			
	50 51 53			122 125			
	55 57 58			126 129			
	59 62 63			132 136			
	64 65 66			138 140			
	67 68 70			141 143			
	71 73 77			144 145			
	78 81 85			146			
	86 89 90						
	92 94 97						
	101 104						
	105 106						
	109 110						
	115 117						
	118 120						
	123 134						
	135 137						
	139 142						
	147						
12	68	4	3	35	8	8	9

Some Byzantine	115/138	83.3%
Clearly Byzantine	35/49	71.4%
Some Egyptian	87/138	63.0%
Clearly Egyptian	12/56	21.4%
Some "Western"	23/138	16.7%
Clearly "Western"	8/69	11.6%

Family 1739 in Acts

Table 40
322

E	EB	EBW	EW	B	BW	W	O/S
22 27 31	1 2 4	5 16 52	9 108	3 11 14	10 35 43	24 26 56	33 34 38
32 36 42	6 7 8	69 130	112	15 17 20	91 93 95	60 61 72	47 103
74 83 88	12 13 18			21 54 80	96 98	76 82 84	124 135
116 132	19 23 25			87 99	100 107	102 109	139 142
145	28 29 30			111 113	114	133	
	37 39 40			119 121			
	41 44 45			122 125			
	46 48 49			126 127			
	50 51 53			128 129			
	55 57 58			131 136			
	59 62 63			138 140			
	64 65 66			141 143			
	67 68 70			144 146			
	71 73 75						
	77 78 79						
	81 85 86						
	89 90 92						
	94 97						
	101 104						
	105 106						
	110 115						
	117 118						
	120 123						
	134 137						
	147						
12	**66**	**5**	**3**	**29**	**11**	**12**	**9**

Some Byzantine	111/138	80.4%
Clearly Byzantine	29/49	59.2%
Some Egyptian	86/138	62.3%
Clearly Egyptian	12/56	21.4%
Some "Western"	31/138	22.5%
Clearly "Western"	12/70	17.1%

Table 41
323

E	EB	EBW	EW	B	BW	W	O/S
22 27 31	1 2 4	5 16 52	9 20	3 11 14	35 43 91	24 26 56	10 21 33
32 36 42	6 7 8	69 130	108 112	15 17 54	93 95 96	60 61 72	34 38 47
74 83 88	12 13 18			80 87 99	98 100	76 82 84	103 124
116 126	19 23 25			111 113	107 114	102 109	135 139
132 145	28 29 30			119 121		133	142
	37 39 40			122 125			
	41 44 45			127 128			
	46 48 49			129 131			
	50 51 53			136 138			
	55 57 58			140 141			
	59 62 63			143 144			
	64 65 66			146			
	67 68 70						
	71 73 75						
	77 78 79						
	81 85 86						
	89 90 92						
	94 97						
	101 104						
	105 106						
	110 115						
	117 118						
	120 123						
	134 137						
	147						
13	**66**	**5**	**4**	**26**	**10**	**12**	**11**

Some Byzantine	107/136	78.7%
Clearly Byzantine	26/49	53.1%
Some Egyptian	88/136	64.7%
Clearly Egyptian	13/56	23.2%
Some "Western"	31/136	22.7%
Clearly "Western"	12/70	17.1%

Family 1739 in Acts

Table 42
429

E	EB	EBW	EW	B	BW	W	O/S
21 22 27	1 2 6	5 16	108 112	9 11 14	35 43 91	24 56 60	3 4 10
31 32 36	7 8 12	130	113 127	15 17 20	95 98	61 76 82	33 34 38
72 74 83	13 18 19			42 69 80		84 102	47 52 54
93 96	23 25 26			87 88		133	75 99
100 114	28 29 30			111 119			103 107
116 128	37 39 40			121 122			124
131	41 44 45			125 126			
	46 48 49			129 132			
	50 51 53			136 138			
	55 57 58			140 141			
	59 62 63			143 144			
	64 65 66			145 146			
	67 68 70						
	71 73 77						
	78 79 81						
	85 86 89						
	90 92 94						
	97 101						
	104 105						
	106 109						
	110 115						
	117 118						
	120 123						
	134 135						
	137 139						
	142 147						
16	**69**	**3**	**4**	**31**	**5**	**9**	**14**

Some Byzantine	104/133	78.2%
Clearly Byzantine	27/48	56.3%
Some Egyptian	92/133	69.2%
Clearly Egyptian	16/55	29.1%
Some "Western"	21/133	15.8%
Clearly "Western"	9/69	13.0%

Table 43
453

E	EB	EBW	EW	B	BW	W	O/S
16 21 22	4 6 7	5 52	108 112	3 9 11	10	24 26 56	1 2 33
27 31 32	8 12 13	103 124	113 127	14 15 17		60 61 84	34 35 38
36 43 54	18 19 23	130		20 42 80		102 133	47 59 74
72 83 88	25 28 29			87 111			79 95 99
91 93 96	30 37 39			119 121			116 118
98 100	40 41 44			122 129			135 139
107 114	45 46 48			132 136			145
125 126	49 50 51			140 141			
128 131	53 55 57			143 144			
138	58 62 63			146			
	64 65 66						
	67 68 69						
	70 71 73						
	75 76 77						
	78 81 82						
	85 86 89						
	90 92 94						
	97 101						
	104 105						
	106 109						
	110 115						
	117 120						
	123 134						
	137 142						
	147						
24	**66**	**5**	**4**	**22**	**1**	**8**	**17**

Some Byzantine	94/130	72.3%
Clearly Byzantine	22/47	46.8%
Some Egyptian	99/130	76.2%
Clearly Egyptian	24/53	45.3%
Some "Western"	18/130	13.8%
Clearly "Western"	8/69	11.6%

Table 44
522

E	EB	EBW	EW	B	BW	W	O/S
14 21 22	1 2 4	5 16	112 113	3 9 11	35 43 91	24 56 60	10 33 34
27 31 32	6 7 8	130	127	15 17 20	95 98	61 76 82	38 47 52
36 72 74	12 13 18			42 69 80		84 102	54 75 99
83 88 93	19 23 25			87 111		133	103 107
96 100	26 28 29			119 121			108 109
116 128	30 37 39			122 125			114 124
131	40 41 44			126 129			143
	45 46 48			132 136			
	49 50 51			138 140			
	53 55 57			141 144			
	58 59 62			145 146			
	63 64 65						
	66 67 68						
	70 71 73						
	77 78 79						
	81 85 86						
	89 90 92						
	94 97						
	101 104						
	105 106						
	110 115						
	117 118						
	120 123						
	134 135						
	137 139						
	142 147						
17	**69**	**3**	**3**	**25**	**5**	**9**	**16**

Some Byzantine	102/131	77.9%
Clearly Byzantine	25/47	53.2%
Some Egyptian	92/131	70.2%
Clearly Egyptian	17/52	32.7%
Some "Western"	20/131	15.3%
Clearly "Western"	9/69	13.0%

Table 45
630

E	EB	EBW	EW	B	BW	W	O/S
14 21 22	1 2 4	5 52	108 112	3 9 11	10 35 43	24 56 60	16 33 34
27 31 36	6 7 8	130	113 127	15 17 20	95 98	61 76 82	38 47 54
42 72 74	12 13 18			69 80 87	100	84 102	59 63 75
83 88 91	19 23 25			111 119		133	99 103
93 96	26 28 29			121 122			107 124
114 116	30 32 37			125 126			135 139
128 131	39 40 41			129 136			140 142
132 138	44 45 46			146			
141 143	48 49 50						
144 145	51 53 55						
	57 58 62						
	64 65 66						
	67 68 70						
	71 73 77						
	78 79 81						
	85 86 89						
	90 92 94						
	97 101						
	104 105						
	106 109						
	110 115						
	117 118						
	120 123						
	134 137						
	147						
24	**66**	**3**	**4**	**18**	**6**	**9**	**17**

Some Byzantine	93/130	71.5%
Clearly Byzantine	18/49	36.7%
Some Egyptian	97/130	74.6%
Clearly Egyptian	24/54	44.4%
Some "Western"	22/130	16.9%
Clearly "Western"	9/69	13.0%

Table 46
945

E	EB	EBW	EW	B	BW	W	O/S
14 21 22	1 2 4	5 52	20 108	3 9 11	10 35 43	24 26 56	16 33 34
27 31 32	6 7 8	130	112 113	15 17 69	95 114	60 61 76	38 47 54
36 42 72	12 13 18		127	80 87		82 102	75 84 99
74 83 88	19 23 25			111 119		109 133	103 107
91 93 96	28 29 30			121 122			124 135
98 100	37 39 40			125 126			139 140
116 128	41 44 45			129			142
131 132	46 48 49						
136 138	50 51 53						
141 143	55 57 58						
144 145	59 62 63						
146	64 65 66						
	67 68 70						
	71 73 77						
	78 79 81						
	85 86 89						
	90 92 94						
	97 101						
	104 105						
	106 110						
	115 117						
	118 120						
	123 134						
	137 147						
28	**65**	**3**	**5**	**15**	**5**	**10**	**16**

Some Byzantine	88/131	67.2%
Clearly Byzantine	15/49	30.6%
Some Egyptian	101/131	77.1%
Clearly Egyptian	28/55	50.9%
Some "Western"	23/131	17.6%
Clearly "Western"	10/69	14.5%

Table 47
1704

E	EB	EBW	EW	B	BW	W	O/S
14 17 21	1 2 4	5 16 52	20 108	3 9 11	10 35 43	24 26 56	33 34 38
22 27 31	6 7 8	130	112 113	15 69 80	95 114	60 61 76	47 54 75
32 36 42	12 13 18			87 111		82 84	99 103
72 74 83	19 23 25			119 121		102 109	107 124
88 91 93	28 29 30			122 125		133	135 139
96 98	37 39 40			126 129			140 142
100 116	41 44 45			132 146			
127 128	46 48 49						
131 136	50 51 53						
138 141	55 57 58						
143 144	59 62 63						
145	64 65 66						
	67 68 70						
	71 73 77						
	78 79 81						
	85 86 89						
	90 92 94						
	97 101						
	104 105						
	106 110						
	115 117						
	118 120						
	123 134						
	137 147						
28	**65**	**4**	**4**	**16**	**5**	**11**	**14**

Some Byzantine	90/133	67.7%
Clearly Byzantine	16/49	32.6%
Some Egyptian	101/133	75.9%
Clearly Egyptian	28/56	50.0%
Some "Western"	24/133	18.0%
Clearly "Western"	11/70	15.7%

Table 48
1739

E	EB	EBW	EW	B	BW	W	O/S
14 21 22	2　4　　6	5　16　52	9　　　20	3　　11 15	35 43 95	24 26 56	1　10　33
27 31 32	7　8　　12	69　　130	108　112	17 80 87		60 61 76	34 38 47
36 42 54	13 18 19		113　127	111　119		82　　84	75　　99
72 74 83	23 25 28			121　122		102　109	103　107
88 91 93	29 30 37			125　126		133	124　135
96　　98	39 40 41			129			139　140
100　114	44 45 46						142
116　128	48 49 50						
131　132	51 53 55						
136　138	57 58 59						
141　143	62 63 64						
144　145	65 66 67						
146	68 70 71						
	73 77 78						
	79 81 85						
	86 89 90						
	92 94 97						
	101　104						
	105　106						
	110　115						
	117　118						
	120　123						
	134　137						
	147						
30	**64**	**5**	**6**	**13**	**3**	**11**	**15**

Some Byzantine	85/132	64.4%
Clearly Byzantine	13/49	26.5%
Some Egyptian	105/132	79.5%
Clearly Egyptian	30/56	53.6%
Some "Western"	25/132	18.9%
Clearly "Western"	11/70	15.7%

Table 49
1891

E	EB	EBW	EW	B	BW	W	O/S
14 21 22	8 12 13	16 52 69	9 20	11 15 17	35 43 95	24 26 56	1 2 3
27 31 32	18 19 23	130	108 112	54 80 87		60 61 76	4 5 6
36 42 72	25 28 29		113 127	111 119		82 84	7 10 33
74 83 88	30 37 39			121 122		102 133	34 38 47
91 93 96	40 41 44			125 126			75 99
98 100	45 46 48			129			103 107
114 116	49 50 51						124 135
128 131	53 55 57						139 140
132 136	58 59 62						142
138 141	63 64 65						
143 144	66 67 68						
145 146	70 71 73						
	77 78 79						
	81 85 86						
	89 90 92						
	94 97						
	101 104						
	105 106						
	109 110						
	115 117						
	118 120						
	123 134						
	137 147						
29	61	4	6	13	3	10	21

Some Byzantine	81/126	64.2%	
Clearly Byzantine	13/48	27.1%	
Some Egyptian	100/126	79.4%	
Clearly Egyptian	29/55	52.7%	
Some "Western"	23/126	18.3%	
Clearly "Western"	10/66	15.2%	

Table 50
2200

E	EB	EBW	EW	B	BW	W	O/S
14 22 27	1 2 4	5 16 52	108 112	3 9 11	10 35 36	24 56 60	6 20 33
31 32 42	7 8 12		113	15 17 21	43 95 98	61 76 82	34 38 47
72 74 83	13 18 19			69 80 87		84 102	54 59 75
88 91 93	23 25 26			99 111		133	103 107
96 100	28 29 30			136 146			117 118
114 116	37 39 40						119 120
132 138	41 44 45						121 122
141 143	46 48 49						123 124
144 145	50 51 53						125 126
	55 57 58						127 128
	62 63 64						129 130
	65 66 67						131 135
	68 70 71						140 142
	73 77 78						
	79 81 85						
	86 89 90						
	92 94 97						
	101 104						
	105 106						
	109 110						
	115 134						
	137 139						
	147						
22	62	3	3	13	6	9	29

Some Byzantine	84/118	71.2%
Clearly Byzantine	13/39	33.3%
Some Egyptian	90/118	76.3%
Clearly Egyptian	22/46	47.8%
Some "Western"	21/117	17.9%
Clearly "Western"	9/63	14.3%

APPENDIX II

The following pages present the percentages of agreement among the ten manuscripts for each chapter of Acts, for different sections, and for the whole document. Included in these charts are B (Codex Vaticanus) and MT (as a representative of the Byzantine tradition) for easy comparison for each manuscript with the Egyptian and Byzantine textual tradition in each chapter and section of Acts. As mentioned on page three (footnote nine), Codex 1739 is not extant for 1:1-2:5.

Acts 1

	B	206	322	323	429	453	522	630	945	1704	1739	1891	2200
206	58.5												
322	52.9	88.2											
323	58.8	88.2	88.2										
429	66.0	92.5	82.4	90.2									
453	58.5	88.7	92.2	82.4	84.9								
522	58.8	82.4	78.4	82.4	88.2	78.4							
630	66.0	84.9	78.4	82.4	92.5	81.1	84.3						
945	66.0	77.4	74.5	86.3	84.9	73.6	76.5	84.9					
1704	62.3	81.1	78.4	86.3	81.1	77.4	72.5	81.1	96.2				
1739													
1891	71.4	71.4	75.0	75.0	78.6	85.7	66.7	92.9	92.9	92.9			
2200	64.2	90.6	84.3	84.3	94.3	86.8	82.4	94.3	83.0	83.0		85.7	
MT	62.3	96.2	90.2	86.3	92.5	92.5	80.4	88.7	77.4	81.1		85.7	94..3

Acts 2

	B	206	322	323	429	453	522	630	945	1704	1739	1891	2200
206	57.1												
322	58.9	87.5											
323	63.4	77.7	88.4										
429	58.9	79.5	81.3	79.5									
453	61.8	68.2	66.4	67.3	60.0								
522	58.9	73.2	75.0	75.9	91.1	58.2							
630	58.6	78.4	81.1	77.5	88.3	63.3	88.3						
945	63.4	75.0	77.7	81.3	86.6	65.5	84.8	85.6					
1704	57.1	81.3	83.0	75.0	82.1	63.6	80.4	88.3	88.4				
1739	68.4	68.4	75.5	81.6	80.6	69.8	79.6	80.4	90.8	81.6			
1891	67.1	74.0	75.3	82.2	78.1	70.4	79.5	81.9	89.0	84.9	94.5		
2200	60.7	78.6	81.3	77.7	85.7	63.6	83.9	89.2	88.4	85.7	81.6	79.5	
MT	58.0	94.6	92.9	81.3	81.3	66.4	74.1	80.2	75.9	83.9	69.4	74.0	81.3

Acts 3

	B	206	322	323	429	453	522	630	945	1704	1739	1891	2200
206	53.4												
322	55.0	79.3											
323	59.3	73.7	91.5										
429	60.0	72.4	81.7	74.6									
453	76.3	61.4	66.1	69.0	67.8								
522	55.0	74.1	76.7	69.5	90.0	62.7							
630	55.2	77.6	79.3	71.9	87.9	68.4	86.2						
945	65.0	69.0	78.3	71.2	88.3	71.2	83.3	82.8					
1704	61.7	72.4	78.3	71.2	85.0	67.8	83.3	86.2	96.7				
1739	66.7	72.4	81.7	74.6	93.3	74.6	86.7	87.9	95.0	91.7			
1891	61.0	78.9	83.1	75.9	93.2	67.8	91.5	89.5	89.8	89.8	93.2		
2200	60.0	72.4	78.3	71.2	90.0	67.8	83.3	87.9	88.3	88.3	93.3	86.4	
MT	55.0	94.8	76.7	74.6	70.0	62.7	73.3	75.9	66.7	70.0	70.0	78.0	70.0

Acts 4

	B	206	322	323	429	453	522	630	945	1704	1739	1891	2200
206	59.1												
322	58.0	82.8											
323	62.9	77.3	89.8										
429	59.6	79.5	78.4	79.8									
453	62.9	76.1	73.9	77.5	74.2								
522	62.5	78.2	78.2	79.5	89.8	70.5							
630	59.6	72.3	70.2	74.5	78.7	70.2	78.7						
945	64.0	76.1	73.9	77.5	73.0	73.0	73.9	78.7					
1704	55.1	75.0	76.8	73.9	71.0	66.7	70.6	64.5	89.9				
1739	68.5	77.3	78.4	84.3	76.4	76.4	77.3	83.0	93.3	82.6			
1891	68.5	77.3	73.9	79.8	76.4	80.9	79.5	83.0	89.9	84.1	93.3		
2200	60.7	75.0	77.3	76.4	76.4	73.0	76.1	85.1	84.3	73.9	85.4	80.9	
MT	59.6	92.0	83.0	73.0	76.4	74.2	78.4	66.0	70.8	75.4	68.5	73.0	68.5

Acts 5

	B	206	322	323	429	453	522	630	945	1704	1739	1891	2200
206	58.2												
322	63.3	84.7											
323	65.3	82.7	91.8										
429	68.4	77.6	79.6	77.6									
453	67.3	65.3	70.4	72.4	77.6								
522	61.2	70.4	74.5	70.4	88.8	74.5							
630	64.9	74.2	79.4	75.3	88.7	74.2	84.5						
945	70.1	79.4	79.4	83.5	88.7	75.3	81.4	83.3					
1704	63.0	77.8	81.5	84.0	81.5	71.6	77.8	78.8	92.5				
1739	72.2	75.3	79.4	81.4	90.7	75.3	85.6	85.4	91.8	87.5			
1891	70.1	73.2	79.4	81.4	83.5	79.4	78.4	82.3	88.7	85.0	90.7		
2200	67.3	79.6	76.5	72.4	86.7	76.5	83.7	87.6	86.6	80.2	86.6	86.6	
MT	59.2	85.7	88.8	84.7	78.6	70.4	75.5	79.4	74.2	79.0	72.2	74.2	77.6

Acts 6

	B	206	322	323	429	453	522	630	945	1704	1739	1891	2200
206	84.6												
322	89.7	89.7											
323	87.2	87.2	97.4										
429	89.7	92.3	94.9	92.3									
453	84.6	82.1	84.6	87.2	87.2								
522	87.2	89.7	92.3	89.7	94.9	87.2							
630	92.3	87.2	92.3	89.7	92.3	87.2	94.9						
945	82.1	76.9	82.1	84.6	82.1	82.1	84.6	89.7					
1704	82.1	76.9	82.1	84.6	82.1	87.2	84.6	89.7	94.9				
1739	87.2	82.1	87.2	89.7	87.2	87.2	89.7	94.9	94.9	94.9			
1891	87.2	82.1	87.2	89.7	87.2	87.2	84.6	89.7	89.7	89.7	94.9		
2200	92.3	87.2	92.3	89.7	92.3	87.2	94.9	100	89.7	89.7	94.9	89.7	
MT	79.5	94.9	84.6	82.1	87.2	82.1	84.6	82.1	71.8	76.9	76.9	82.1	82.1

Acts 7

	B	206	322	323	429	453	522	630	945	1704	1739	1891	2200
206	61.7												
322	58.6	83.8											
323	61.1	76.0	89.2										
429	60.5	79.2	84.7	84.1									
453	66.9	68.2	70.1	75.2	70.7								
522	60.5	79.2	83.4	82.8	88.5	75.2							
630	63.7	77.3	83.4	87.9	89.2	73.9	89.2						
945	61.8	74.7	82.2	87.9	87.9	74.5	89.2	94.9					
1704	67.3	79.8	82.2	86.0	86.0	73.8	86.9	93.5	93.5				
1739	62.4	74.0	82.8	87.3	86.0	72.6	87.3	93.0	98.1	90.7			
1891	60.0	74.1	78.7	83.3	84.0	72.0	85.3	90.7	95.3	90.3	94.7		
2200	76.5	80.0	82.4	86.3	84.3	84.3	84.3	100	96.1	94.1	94.1	93.9	
MT	62.4	92.2	82.2	77.7	78.3	72.0	78.3	77.7	76.4	82.2	75.8	75.3	82.4

Acts 8

	B	206	322	323	429	453	522	630	945	1704	1739	1891	2200
206	67.7												
322	69.8	85.4											
323	72.9	83.3	92.7										
429	77.1	81.3	87.5	87.5									
453	81.7	75.3	79.6	82.8	87.1								
522	75.0	79.2	82.3	84.4	93.8	87.1							
630	80.2	80.2	86.5	86.5	93.8	89.2	89.6						
945	76.8	74.7	81.1	83.2	88.4	87.0	84.2	88.4					
1704	72.6	75.8	84.2	86.3	90.5	83.7	84.2	88.4	95.8				
1739	78.1	79.2	84.4	86.5	89.6	89.2	87.5	89.6	90.5	88.4			
1891	79.1	81.3	86.8	90.1	92.3	92.0	90.1	92.3	94.4	93.3	96.7		
2200	77.1	81.3	84.4	80.2	87.5	84.9	87.5	91.7	84.2	82.1	85.4	89.0	
MT	69.8	95.8	85.4	81.3	81.3	75.3	79.2	82.3	74.7	75.8	77.1	79.1	83.3

Acts 9

	206	322	323	429	453	522	630	945	1704	1739	1891	2200
206	55.7											
322	58.3	75.7										
323	60.0	71.3	94.8									
429	68.7	75.7	67.8	67.0								
453	73.9	63.5	67.8	67.0	73.0							
522	67.0	72.2	64.3	63.5	94.8	69.6						
630	68.7	75.7	65.2	64.3	91.3	72.2	91.3					
945	62.6	59.1	67.0	69.6	77.4	64.3	73.9	74.8				
1704	60.9	65.2	73.0	72.2	79.1	64.3	75.7	74.8	91.3			
1739	70.4	66.1	72.2	73.9	86.1	72.2	82.6	83.5	91.3	87.8		
1891	72.2	67.0	70.4	72.2	89.6	73.9	86.1	86.1	87.8	84.3	96.5	
2200	65.2	76.5	65.2	66.1	87.0	67.0	85.2	90.4	72.2	77.4	79.1	81.7
MT	54.8	91.3	77.4	72.2	69.6	61.7	66.1	71.3	53.9	60.0	60.9	61.7	72.2
B	206	322	323	429	453	522	630	945	1704	1739	1891	2200

Acts 10

	206	322	323	429	453	522	630	945	1704	1739	1891	2200
206	64.1											
322	66.4	81.3										
323	71.1	75.0	90.6									
429	64.1	71.1	75.0	76.6								
453	77.3	67.2	71.9	76.6	74.2							
522	63.3	68.0	75.0	76.6	87.5	72.7						
630	67.2	67.2	75.0	79.7	89.8	75.8	87.5					
945	69.5	68.8	77.3	81.3	80.5	75.0	83.6	85.2				
1704	68.0	75.0	78.9	81.3	83.6	75.0	85.2	86.7	93.8			
1739	75.0	68.0	76.6	81.3	84.4	78.9	85.9	89.1	93.0	91.4		
1891	70.9	66.1	74.8	79.5	90.6	77.2	87.4	93.7	89.8	88.2	93.7	
2200	68.8	68.0	75.8	75.8	87.5	75.8	87.5	90.6	83.6	85.2	87.5	92.1
MT	64.8	95.3	85.2	77.3	71.9	67.2	68.8	68.0	69.5	74.2	68.8	66.9	70.3
B	206	322	323	429	453	522	630	945	1704	1739	1891	2200

Acts 11

	206	322	323	429	453	522	630	945	1704	1739	1891	2200
206	52.6											
322	46.1	76.3										
323	52.6	69.7	92.1									
429	61.8	77.6	78.9	75.0								
453	75.0	71.1	64.5	61.8	76.3							
522	60.5	77.6	80.3	76.3	93.4	76.3						
630	57.9	75.0	77.6	76.3	86.8	73.7	90.8					
945	59.5	71.6	70.3	67.6	89.2	74.3	82.4	82.4				
1704	55.6	75.0	79.2	72.2	88.9	72.2	88.9	81.9	92.9			
1739	70.7	65.3	68.0	74.7	84.0	72.0	80.0	81.3	84.9	74.6		
1891	71.1	65.8	68.4	72.4	86.8	75.0	82.9	86.8	85.1	77.8	94.7	
2200	61.8	76.3	75.0	73.7	88.2	73.7	89.5	90.8	82.4	83.3	80.0	85.5
MT	51.3	85.5	82.9	75.0	75.0	69.7	76.3	73.7	68.9	76.4	61.3	61.8
B	206	322	323	429	453	522	630	945	1704	1739	1891	2200

(MT column 2200: 73.7)

Acts 12

	206	322	323	429	453	522	630	945	1704	1739	1891	2200
206	64.2											
322	68.7	71.6										
323	71.6	74.6	94.0									
429	67.2	92.5	68.7	71.6								
453	68.7	71.6	65.7	71.6	74.6							
522	64.2	94.0	68.7	68.7	92.5	68.7						
630	68.7	85.1	68.7	74.6	85.1	77.6	85.1					
945	67.2	89.6	68.7	74.6	89.6	77.6	89.6	92.5				
1704	67.2	85.1	77.6	74.6	85.1	74.6	88.1	85.1	91.0			
1739	76.1	82.1	77.6	80.6	82.1	77.6	82.1	91.0	88.1	88.1		
1891	71.6	86.6	70.1	76.1	86.6	79.1	86.6	95.5	94.0	86.6	92.5	
2200	71.6	83.6	74.6	74.6	83.6	76.1	83.6	91.0	88.1	89.6	94.0	94.0
MT	64.2	68.7	88.1	85.1	68.7	68.7	65.7	67.2	68.7	74.6	70.1	70.1
B	206	322	323	429	453	522	630	945	1704	1739	1891	2200

(MT column 2200: 73.1)

Acts 13

206	69.4												
322	68.7	81.5											
323	68.8	83.2	92.4										
429	70.3	91.2	76.2	81.9									
453	78.2	76.7	77.4	79.0	76.2								
522	67.1	90.3	78.6	81.7	91.1	74.5							
630	68.9	89.8	81.6	84.7	90.5	76.9	91.1						
945	70.9	93.2	78.2	82.6	93.9	79.6	92.5	91.9					
1704	67.3	91.8	80.1	83.2	93.2	76.7	90.3	91.8	96.6				
1739	73.0	90.5	79.6	82.6	91.2	79.6	89.0	89.9	94.6	91.2			
1891	72.3	92.5	79.6	82.6	93.2	81.0	91.8	92.6	98.0	94.6	95.9		
2200	66.9	90.5	81.0	84.0	91.2	74.8	91.1	96.6	91.2	92.5	87.8	90.5	
MT	62.2	74.1	82.3	81.9	69.6	68.7	70.5	73.0	69.6	71.4	69.6	69.6	75.0
	B	206	322	323	429	453	522	630	945	1704	1739	1891	2200

Acts 14

206	61.8												
322	60.4	73.0											
323	60.4	70.8	86.8										
429	67.0	89.9	74.7	72.5									
453	81.3	68.5	65.9	68.1	70.3								
522	61.1	89.9	68.9	71.1	87.8	67.8							
630	60.7	82.8	71.9	69.7	82.0	71.9	81.8						
945	67.0	87.6	70.3	74.7	86.8	74.7	86.7	91.0					
1704	60.4	85.4	79.1	74.7	84.6	70.3	82.2	84.3	91.2				
1739	69.2	78.7	71.4	76.9	80.2	79.1	78.9	86.5	89.0	82.4			
1891	69.2	84.3	69.2	75.8	83.5	76.9	83.3	87.6	94.5	85.7	93.4		
2200	65.5	78.8	71.3	72.4	78.2	74.7	77.9	94.3	90.8	83.9	85.1	86.2	
MT	67.0	69.7	89.0	81.3	73.6	70.3	65.6	67.4	71.4	78.0	71.4	71.4	71.3
	B	206	322	323	429	453	522	630	945	1704	1739	1891	2200

Acts 15

206	64.9												
322	64.9	77.4											
323	65.8	78.3	95.7										
429	63.2	91.3	80.0	82.6									
453	76.3	72.2	73.9	74.8	72.2								
522	64.0	92.2	78.3	80.9	95.7	73.0							
630	67.3	87.7	80.7	83.3	93.0	76.3	92.1						
945	63.2	88.7	78.3	80.9	92.2	72.2	93.0	91.2					
1704	62.3	90.4	78.3	82.6	90.4	71.3	91.3	87.7	95.7				
1739	66.7	88.7	80.0	82.6	88.7	75.7	87.8	91.2	88.7	88.7			
1891	69.3	90.4	82.6	85.2	90.4	78.3	89.6	91.2	90.4	91.3	97.4		
2200	65.8	90.4	84.3	85.2	93.9	74.8	89.6	93.0	90.4	89.6	92.2	94.8	
MT	67.5	74.8	90.4	87.8	77.4	75.7	75.7	78.9	75.7	75.7	76.5	79.1	80.9
	B	206	322	323	429	453	522	630	945	1704	1739	1891	2200

Acts 16

206	59.3												
322	54.5	67.2											
323	55.6	69.9	94.3										
429	61.6	90.3	73.4	75.2									
453	76.0	75.0	70.2	72.0	76.2								
522	60.2	91.1	71.3	69.9	86.3	75.8							
630	65.0	87.1	73.0	72.4	85.5	81.5	84.7						
945	66.9	79.7	75.6	76.6	83.2	81.6	80.5	84.6					
1704	59.2	75.8	76.6	74.4	81.0	75.4	78.2	81.5	92.8				
1739	75.2	79.8	73.4	74.4	82.5	87.3	79.0	86.3	89.6	81.7			
1891	70.4	85.5	72.6	73.6	85.7	84.9	81.5	93.5	89.6	83.3	91.3		
2200	65.3	86.3	74.8	74.2	84.8	80.8	83.9	96.0	83.9	80.8	86.4	91.2	
MT	52.8	65.3	96.0	92.8	71.4	69.0	68.5	70.2	72.0	73.0	69.8	69.8	72.0
	B	206	322	323	429	453	522	630	945	1704	1739	1891	2200

Acts 17

	B	206	322	323	429	453	522	630	945	1704	1739	1891	2200
206	65.8												
322	62.4	73.5											
323	62.9	74.1	91.4										
429	65.0	92.3	74.4	73.3									
453	71.3	68.7	64.3	66.7	69.6								
522	63.2	88.9	74.4	73.3	89.7	66.1							
630	70.1	83.8	76.9	77.6	82.9	73.9	82.9						
945	72.6	81.2	70.9	75.0	78.6	67.8	76.9	80.3					
1704	67.5	82.9	75.2	77.6	82.1	67.8	80.3	80.3	93.2				
1739	79.5	84.6	77.8	81.9	82.1	73.0	80.3	87.2	93.2	88.0			
1891	76.9	85.5	75.2	79.3	84.6	72.2	81.2	88.0	90.6	85.5	97.4		
2200	69.2	86.3	81.2	80.2	90.6	72.2	82.1	90.6	79.5	82.9	86.3	88.9	
MT	64.1	67.5	83.8	75.9	71.8	67.0	71.8	71.8	65.8	70.1	70.9	70.1	77.8

Acts 18

	B	206	322	323	429	453	522	630	945	1704	1739	1891	2200
206	66.3												
322	60.5	75.0											
323	61.7	76.3	91.4										
429	66.7	93.8	72.8	76.5									
453	66.7	66.3	69.1	71.6	67.9								
522	62.5	91.3	68.8	71.3	93.8	62.5							
630	67.9	83.8	75.3	79.0	88.9	70.4	82.5						
945	72.8	82.5	71.6	76.5	82.7	75.3	78.8	84.0					
1704	72.8	78.8	76.5	74.1	81.5	77.8	75.0	82.7	95.1				
1739	72.8	85.0	74.1	79.0	85.2	74.1	81.3	86.4	92.6	87.7			
1891	72.8	85.0	75.3	80.2	87.7	74.1	83.8	88.9	92.6	87.7	95.1		
2200	66.7	82.5	76.5	77.8	84.0	69.1	77.5	86.4	81.5	82.7	84.0	84.0	
MT	59.3	67.5	87.7	86.4	65.4	66.7	61.3	67.9	63.0	67.9	65.4	66.7	74.1

Acts 19

	206	322	323	429	453	522	630	945	1704	1739	1891	2200	
206	68.6												
322	68.6	75.2											
323	67.9	76.6	94.2										
429	69.3	93.4	76.6	78.1									
453	78.1	79.6	74.5	75.9	78.8								
522	64.7	93.1	75.5	78.4	88.2	75.5							
630	72.1	94.1	73.5	75.0	92.6	83.1	87.1						
945	74.5	92.7	73.0	74.5	89.8	80.3	87.3	91.9					
1704	70.1	91.2	74.5	74.5	88.3	78.8	89.2	89.0	95.6				
1739	75.9	89.8	71.5	73.0	86.9	80.3	85.3	90.4	97.1	92.7			
1891	74.5	92.7	71.5	73.0	89.8	81.8	87.3	94.9	97.1	92.7	95.6		
2200	70.1	92.7	75.2	75.2	90.5	82.5	87.3	94.1	88.3	88.3	86.9	91.2	
MT	65.7	75.2	90.5	87.6	75.2	72.3	76.5	72.1	70.1	73.0	68.6	68.6	76.6
B	206	322	323	429	453	522	630	945	1704	1739	1891	2200	

Acts 20

	206	322	323	429	453	522	630	945	1704	1739	1891	2200	
206	60.5												
322	61.2	76.0											
323	63.7	74.2	94.2										
429	60.5	91.9	72.7	71.8									
453	69.7	67.2	68.9	68.9	68.0								
522	63.2	94.0	77.2	77.8	89.7	69.6							
630	63.7	95.2	75.2	75.0	90.3	68.9	94.9						
945	64.5	87.1	77.7	79.0	84.7	68.0	86.3	87.9					
1704	59.3	87.0	80.8	78.9	82.9	64.5	85.3	86.2	93.5				
1739	68.5	87.1	79.3	80.6	84.7	73.8	85.5	89.5	94.4	87.8			
1891	62.1	93.5	74.4	74.2	88.7	68.9	91.5	95.2	87.9	86.2	91.1		
2200	69.4	89.8	66.7	67.3	85.7	72.3	90.5	93.9	77.6	79.6	83.7	95.9	
MT	64.5	65.3	87.6	83.1	69.4	66.4	72.6	67.7	69.4	69.1	69.4	63.7	57.1
B	206	322	323	429	453	522	630	945	1704	1739	1891	2200	

Acts 21

	B	206	322	323	429	453	522	630	945	1704	1739	1891	2200
206	64.5												
322	58.2	67.3											
323	55.5	69.1	93.6										
429	67.3	93.6	66.4	68.2									
453	77.3	70.9	64.5	67.3	71.8								
522	61.8	89.1	60.9	62.7	90.0	65.5							
630	70.0	90.9	67.3	68.2	90.9	74.5	86.4						
945	68.2	85.5	62.7	65.5	85.5	70.9	80.9	90.9					
1704	63.4	80.5	65.9	68.3	80.5	73.2	70.7	82.9	90.2				
1739	70.0	86.4	60.9	63.6	86.4	72.7	81.8	91.8	93.6	85.4			
1891	67.3	87.3	64.5	67.3	87.3	70.0	84.5	92.7	88.2	78.0	89.1		
2200	65.1	88.0	66.3	67.5	86.7	71.1	84.3	92.8	85.5	80.5	85.5	89.2	
MT	58.2	62.7	89.1	87.3	64.5	68.2	60.0	62.7	56.4	61.0	58.2	60.9	62.7

Acts 22

	B	206	322	323	429	453	522	630	945	1704	1739	1891	2200
206	75.5												
322	74.5	77.9											
323	71.0	74.5	91.5										
429	75.5	93.7	80.0	76.6									
453	79.6	80.9	75.5	71.0	80.9								
522	74.5	91.6	72.6	70.2	90.5	81.9							
630	76.6	90.5	76.8	75.5	90.5	81.9	85.3						
945	75.5	87.4	70.5	71.3	84.2	72.3	82.1	81.1					
1704	69.9	88.1	72.6	72.3	83.3	72.3	83.3	83.3	90.5				
1739	77.7	86.3	71.6	75.5	84.2	74.5	81.1	85.3	92.6	85.7			
1891	74.5	91.6	74.7	72.3	89.5	79.8	85.3	90.5	88.4	85.7	92.6		
2200	77.7	91.6	80.0	77.7	91.6	85.1	86.3	91.6	82.1	82.1	84.2	89.5	
MT	73.4	73.7	89.5	85.1	75.8	75.5	72.6	76.8	66.3	71.4	67.4	70.5	74.7

Acts 23

	B	206	322	323	429	453	522	630	945	1704	1739	1891	2200
206	64.7												
322	62.7	70.6											
323	59.4	72.3	89.1										
429	64.7	94.1	70.6	72.3									
453	68.6	70.6	73.5	68.3	70.6								
522	65.7	92.2	71.6	69.3	90.2	69.6							
630	67.6	88.2	72.5	68.3	84.3	70.6	86.3						
945	70.6	85.3	70.6	69.3	83.3	71.6	83.3	92.2					
1704	67.6	83.3	74.5	73.3	81.4	69.6	82.4	88.2	94.1				
1739	72.3	88.1	70.3	69.0	86.1	73.3	84.2	91.1	97.0	91.1			
1891	71.6	90.2	72.5	71.3	86.3	75.5	84.3	90.2	93.1	89.2	96.0		
2200	70.6	89.2	75.5	75.2	87.3	79.4	86.3	89.2	88.2	86.3	91.1	91.2	
MT	56.9	66.7	90.2	85.1	68.6	70.6	67.6	67.6	64.7	70.6	64.4	66.7	73.5
	B	206	322	323	429	453	522	630	945	1704	1739	1891	2200

Acts 24

	B	206	322	323	429	453	522	630	945	1704	1739	1891	2200
206	62.1												
322	60.0	79.2											
323	63.7	71.7	91.3										
429	64.2	94.8	78.1	73.9									
453	73.7	68.8	69.8	71.7	69.8								
522	66.3	93.8	78.1	73.9	94.8	70.8							
630	71.6	66.7	69.8	75.0	64.6	74.0	63.5						
945	77.9	58.3	63.5	71.7	58.3	74.0	57.3	88.5					
1704	69.5	62.5	70.8	79.3	62.5	69.8	63.5	81.3	86.5				
1739	81.1	57.3	63.5	71.7	57.3	71.9	57.3	90.6	93.8	82.3			
1891	76.8	59.4	63.5	71.7	59.4	70.8	59.4	92.7	91.7	82.3	95.8		
2200	71.6	67.7	72.9	75.0	67.7	70.8	66.7	90.6	83.3	80.2	85.4	87.5	
MT	64.2	86.5	87.5	82.6	87.5	72.9	86.5	65.6	60.4	68.8	59.4	59.4	66.7
	B	206	322	323	429	453	522	630	945	1704	1739	1891	2200

Acts 25

	B	206	322	323	429	453	522	630	945	1704	1739	1891	2200
206	55.1												
322	57.1	82.7											
323	61.2	77.6	86.7										
429	58.2	95.9	83.7	78.6									
453	64.3	72.4	76.5	73.5	74.5								
522	56.1	93.9	78.6	75.5	93.9	73.5							
630	68.4	68.4	75.5	74.5	66.3	72.4	63.3						
945	68.4	62.2	71.4	72.4	64.3	70.4	61.2	89.8					
1704	64.3	71.4	77.6	78.6	74.5	74.5	70.4	85.7	89.8				
1739	69.1	62.9	72.2	75.3	64.9	72.2	63.9	90.7	94.8	88.7			
1891	70.1	62.9	72.2	76.3	64.9	73.2	63.9	90.7	93.8	86.6	95.8		
2200	69.4	68.4	73.5	72.4	68.4	74.5	65.3	94.9	88.8	85.7	89.7	89.7	
MT	58.2	87.8	87.8	79.6	88.8	72.4	85.7	67.3	61.2	71.4	63.9	63.9	67.3
	B	206	322	323	429	453	522	630	945	1704	1739	1891	2200

Acts 26

	B	206	322	323	429	453	522	630	945	1704	1739	1891	2200
206	50.5												
322	58.2	83.5											
323	58.9	76.7	91.1										
429	52.7	93.4	86.8	78.9									
453	61.5	65.9	65.9	66.7	70.3								
522	52.7	93.4	83.5	78.9	92.3	65.9							
630	59.3	56.0	57.1	61.1	52.7	62.6	54.9						
945	61.5	48.4	52.7	55.6	51.6	64.8	48.4	85.7					
1704	54.9	57.1	60.4	56.7	59.3	61.5	54.9	79.1	86.8				
1739	64.8	51.6	56.0	58.9	53.8	67.0	51.6	87.9	94.5	84.6			
1891	62.2	52.2	56.7	58.4	54.4	65.6	51.1	90.0	92.2	85.6	94.4		
2200	53.8	60.4	59.3	53.3	60.4	65.9	58.2	81.3	81.3	84.6	83.5	85.6	
MT	57.1	83.5	90.1	86.7	86.8	67.0	85.7	57.1	51.6	59.3	54.9	54.4	59.3
	B	206	322	323	429	453	522	630	945	1704	1739	1891	2200

Acts 27

	B	206	322	323	429	453	522	630	945	1704	1739	1891	2200
206	64.7												
322	68.9	86.6											
323	70.3	85.6	97.5										
429	65.5	92.4	88.2	87.3									
453	81.5	71.4	76.5	78.8	74.8								
522	66.4	90.8	86.6	85.6	93.3	75.6							
630	77.1	68.6	74.6	73.5	71.2	74.6	69.5						
945	78.2	66.4	73.9	74.6	67.2	78.2	68.1	85.6					
1704	65.5	83.2	88.2	87.3	86.6	74.8	81.5	76.3	75.6				
1739	78.2	60.5	68.1	68.6	63.0	75.6	63.0	83.1	89.1	71.4			
1891	81.5	67.2	74.8	73.7	71.4	79.8	68.1	89.8	90.8	76.5	90.8		
2200	80.7	68.1	75.6	74.6	70.6	79.0	68.9	91.5	88.2	79.0	88.2	94.1	
MT	71.4	86.6	91.6	90.7	89.9	79.0	88.2	74.6	70.6	86.6	65.5	73.1	75.6

Acts 28

	B	206	322	323	429	453	522	630	945	1704	1739	1891	2200
206	61.2												
322	68.4	85.7											
323	65.3	82.7	96.9										
429	63.3	94.9	87.8	84.7									
453	70.8	74.0	81.3	80.2	75.0								
522	62.2	91.8	83.7	82.7	93.9	76.0							
630	60.4	83.3	83.3	80.2	83.3	77.7	78.1						
945	76.5	63.3	72.4	73.5	64.3	72.9	64.3	60.4					
1704	67.3	85.7	92.9	89.8	88.8	82.3	87.8	86.5	67.3				
1739	77.6	57.1	66.3	65.3	58.2	68.8	58.2	57.3	90.8	61.2			
1891	65.3	84.7	86.7	83.7	86.7	80.2	81.6	89.6	63.3	89.8	62.2		
2200	62.5	84.4	87.5	84.4	85.4	80.9	82.3	93.8	64.6	88.5	59.4	89.6	
MT	67.3	86.7	93.9	92.9	87.8	79.2	86.7	85.4	70.4	94.9	65.3	90.8	87.5

Acts 1-6

	B	206	322	323	429	453	522	630	945	1704	1739	1891	2200
206	59.8												
322	61.2	85.2											
323	64.7	80.2	90.6										
429	64.7	80.8	81.7	80.8									
453	66.7	71.9	73.3	74.2	73.0								
522	62.1	76.2	77.6	76.5	90.2	69.7							
630	64.0	78.3	79.9	77.6	88.1	72.1	86.1						
945	67.1	75.8	77.4	80.5	84.0	72.3	80.8	84.2					
1704	61.6	77.9	80.3	78.3	80.4	70.3	78.1	83.1	92.3				
1739	71.0	74.2	79.3	81.9	84.9	75.3	82.7	85.2	92.7	86.4			
1891	69.5	76.1	78.5	81.0	82.5	77.2	81.3	84.9	89.5	86.5	93.0		
2200	65.2	79.5	80.4	77.2	86.3	73.7	83.0	89.9	86.7	83.1	86.9	84.1	
MT	60.5	92.4	86.8	80.1	80.0	72.8	76.8	79.0	73.1	78.5	70.8	75.7	78.0

Acts 7-10

	B	206	322	323	429	453	522	630	945	1704	1739	1891	2200
206	62.1												
322	62.7	81.5											
323	65.7	76.1	91.5										
429	66.5	76.7	78.8	78.8									
453	74.0	68.2	71.8	75.1	75.3								
522	65.5	74.6	76.6	77.0	90.7	75.5							
630	69.0	74.8	77.6	80.0	90.7	76.9	89.3						
945	66.9	69.5	77.2	81.0	83.6	74.6	83.2	86.5					
1704	67.0	73.8	79.3	81.1	84.5	73.8	82.9	85.6	93.5				
1739	70.6	71.6	79.0	82.5	86.3	77.3	85.9	89.1	93.7	89.7			
1891	69.4	71.7	77.2	81.0	88.6	77.5	87.0	90.7	91.9	88.7	95.2		
2200	70.8	75.3	75.6	75.4	86.9	76.5	86.4	92.1	82.0	83.3	85.4	88.5	
MT	62.7	93.5	82.5	77.0	75.2	69.0	73.2	74.6	69.1	72.8	70.8	70.6	75.6

Acts 11-14

	B	206	322	323	429	453	522	630	945	1704	1739	1891	2200
206	63.3												
322	62.2	76.7											
323	64.0	76.0	91.3										
429	67.3	88.4	75.1	76.5									
453	76.6	72.8	70.0	71.6	74.5								
522	63.9	88.3	74.9	75.7	91.0	72.2							
630	64.7	84.4	76.3	77.7	86.8	75.2	87.8						
945	67.1	87.0	73.1	76.3	90.5	77.0	88.6	89.9					
1704	63.4	85.8	79.3	77.5	88.9	73.9	87.7	86.9	93.6				
1739	72.2	81.2	75.0	79.3	85.6	77.6	83.6	87.6	90.2	85.4			
1891	71.2	84.2	73.2	77.8	88.5	78.5	87.1	90.8	93.9	87.8	94.5		
2200	66.4	83.7	76.4	77.5	86.2	74.8	86.4	93.9	88.8	88.2	86.7	89.2	
MT	61.5	74.4	85.0	81.0	71.5	69.3	69.7	70.8	69.7	74.5	68.5	68.6	73.5

Acts 15-19

	B	206	322	323	429	453	522	630	945	1704	1739	1891	2200
206	65.0												
322	62.4	73.6											
323	62.9	75.0	93.5										
429	65.2	92.1	75.6	77.2									
453	74.3	73.0	70.6	72.4	73.5								
522	62.9	91.3	73.9	74.8	90.5	71.1							
630	68.6	87.7	75.8	77.2	88.6	77.7	86.0						
945	70.0	85.3	74.0	76.6	85.6	75.7	83.4	86.7					
1704	66.0	84.3	76.1	76.7	84.9	74.2	83.1	84.4	94.4				
1739	74.2	85.7	75.3	77.9	85.1	78.6	82.7	88.5	92.3	87.8			
1891	72.8	88.1	75.3	77.9	87.7	78.7	84.6	91.6	92.2	88.2	95.3		
2200	67.5	88.1	78.4	78.4	89.0	76.6	84.4	92.5	85.0	85.0	87.3	90.4	
MT	62.0	70.3	89.9	86.2	72.7	70.4	71.2	72.4	69.7	72.2	70.5	71.0	76.3

Acts 20-24

	B	206	322	323	429	453	522	630	945	1704	1739	1891	2200
206	65.1												
322	63.0	74.0											
323	62.4	72.4	92.1										
429	66.1	93.5	73.3	72.4									
453	73.6	71.4	70.2	69.3	71.9								
522	66.0	92.1	72.0	70.8	91.0	71.2							
630	69.5	86.9	72.3	72.4	84.6	73.7	83.8						
945	70.9	81.2	69.3	71.6	79.7	71.2	78.5	88.2					
1704	65.8	80.5	74.3	75.5	78.0	69.1	78.1	84.8	91.3				
1739	73.5	81.6	69.4	72.3	80.2	73.2	78.4	89.7	94.3	86.7			
1891	69.9	85.0	70.0	71.4	82.7	72.7	81.5	92.4	89.8	85.2	92.8		
2200	71.2	84.7	73.1	73.3	83.5	76.3	81.8	91.3	84.0	82.3	86.3	90.1	
MT	63.2	70.4	88.7	84.6	72.7	70.4	71.5	67.9	63.6	69.1	63.9	64.1	68.2

Acts 25-28

	B	206	322	323	429	453	522	630	945	1704	1739	1891	2200
206	58.4												
322	63.5	84.7											
323	64.4	80.9	93.3										
429	60.3	94.1	86.7	82.7									
453	70.3	71.0	75.2	75.1	73.8								
522	59.9	92.4	83.3	80.9	93.3	73.0							
630	67.0	69.2	73.0	72.6	68.7	72.1	66.7						
945	71.7	60.6	68.2	69.6	62.3	72.0	61.1	80.6					
1704	63.3	75.1	80.5	79.0	78.1	73.5	74.4	81.6	79.6				
1739	72.8	58.3	65.9	67.2	60.2	71.2	59.5	79.9	92.1	76.0			
1891	70.5	67.1	73.0	73.4	69.8	75.1	66.6	90.0	85.1	84.2	85.9		
2200	67.6	70.3	74.3	71.6	71.3	75.4	68.8	90.6	81.2	84.2	80.6	90.0	
MT	64.0	86.2	90.9	87.6	88.4	74.8	86.7	71.5	64.0	78.8	62.7	71.0	72.8

Acts 1-14

	B	206	322	323	429	453	522	630	945	1704	1739	1891	2200
206	61.7												
322	62.0	81.4											
323	64.9	77.5	91.1										
429	66.1	81.4	78.7	78.8									
453	72.3	70.8	71.8	73.8	74.3								
522	63.9	79.1	76.5	76.5	90.6	72.6							
630	66.1	78.7	77.9	78.6	88.8	74.9	87.9						
945	67.0	76.7	76.1	79.5	85.7	74.5	83.9	86.8					
1704	64.1	78.8	79.6	79.1	84.5	72.7	82.8	85.2	93.1				
1739	71.2	75.3	77.9	81.4	85.6	76.8	84.2	87.5	92.4	87.3			
1891	70.0	76.9	76.4	80.0	86.7	77.7	85.3	89.1	91.8	87.8	94.3		
2200	67.4	79.5	77.6	76.7	86.5	74.9	85.2	91.9	85.8	84.8	86.3	87.3	
MT	61.6	87.7	84.7	79.2	75.8	70.3	73.4	74.9	70.6	75.2	70.1	71.5	75.9

Acts 15-28

	B	206	322	323	429	453	522	630	945	1704	1739	1891	2200
206	63.2												
322	62.9	76.7											
323	63.1	75.7	93.0										
429	64.2	93.2	77.8	77.0									
453	73.0	71.9	71.7	72.1	73.0								
522	63.2	91.9	75.8	75.1	91.5	71.7							
630	68.5	82.5	73.8	74.3	81.9	74.8	79.9						
945	70.7	77.2	70.8	73.0	77.3	73.2	75.5	85.6					
1704	65.2	80.5	76.8	76.9	80.8	72.4	79.0	83.7	89.2				
1739	73.6	76.9	70.7	73.1	76.7	74.7	74.8	86.6	93.0	84.2			
1891	71.2	81.4	72.8	74.4	81.2	75.7	78.5	91.5	89.4	86.1	91.9		
2200	68.6	82.0	75.6	74.9	82.3	76.2	79.0	91.6	83.6	84.0	85.1	90.2	
MT	63.0	74.6	89.8	86.1	76.9	71.6	75.6	70.6	66.0	73.1	66.1	68.6	72.9

Acts 1-28

	B	206	322	323	429	453	522	630	945	1704	1739	1891	2200
206	62.5												
322	62.5	78.9											
323	64.0	76.5	92.1										
429	65.1	87.7	78.2	77.8									
453	72.7	71.4	71.8	72.9	73.6								
522	63.5	85.8	76.1	75.8	91.1	72.1							
630	67.4	80.8	75.7	76.2	85.1	74.8	83.6						
945	69.0	77.0	73.3	76.0	81.2	73.8	79.5	86.1					
1704	64.7	79.7	78.1	77.9	82.5	72.5	80.8	84.4	91.0				
1739	72.5	76.2	74.0	76.9	80.8	75.7	79.1	87.0	92.7	85.6			
1891	70.6	79.3	74.4	76.9	83.7	76.6	81.6	90.4	90.5	86.9	93.0		
2200	68.0	80.8	76.5	75.7	84.2	75.6	81.9	91.7	84.6	84.4	85.7	88.9	
MT	62.4	80.7	87.4	82.8	76.4	71.0	74.6	72.5	68.2	74.1	67.9	69.9	74.3